Baby, It's You

Messages from Deceased Heroes

Compiled by

Maureen McGill

For permission, serialization, condensation, adaptions, or for our catalog of other publications, write to Ozark Mountain Publishing, LLC. P.O. box 754, Huntsville, AR 72740, ATTN: Permissions Department.

Library of Congress Cataloging-in-Publication Data

McGill, Maureen -1952

Baby, It's You compiled by Maureen McGill

A collection of real life stories and ways connections were made from the spirit world back to their loved ones.

1. Life After Death 2. Metaphysics 3. Spirit World 4. Death

I. McGill, Maureen, 1952 II. Life After Death III. Title

Library of Congress Catalog Card Number: 2015951675

ISBN: 9781940265315

Cover Design: noir33.com

Book set in: Maiandra GD, Lucida Handwriting

Book Design: Tab Pillar

Published by:

PO Box 754

Huntsville, AR 72740

800-935-0045 or 479-738-2348 fax: 479-738-2448

WWW.OZARKMT.COM

Printed in the United States of America

To the memory of my father, Captain George R. McGill, US Army, WWII veteran.

To all the mothers, wives, family members, and surviving heroes who shared their stories with me.

And to my brothers, Commander Robert G. McGill, US Navy and Mr. Richard G. McGill.

Table of Contents

Pictures Credits

Foreword: pg ii – Danica McKellar w/ Bill's camera
An American Soldier: pg 1 – Nadia McCaffrey; pg 7 – Photographer Unknown
Patrick and His Mother, Nadia: pg 12 – Nadia McCaffrey
Robert and Ally: pg 13 & pg 15 – Ally Wheatley
Alan and Amber: pg 16 – Photographer Unknown; pg 18 – Sandy Humphreys
Robert and Holly: pg 19 & pg 22 – Alyssa Pryor/Alyssa Rene Photography
Cameron and Timi: pg 25 – Timi Branum
John and Ann: pg 28 – Free Pixabay Photo
David and Melinda: pg 32 – Photographer Unknown
Kenney and Melissa: pg 33 & pg 35 – Melissa Wilson
Chad and Stephanie: pg 37 – Chad D. Groepper
Shawn and Stephanie: pg 43 – Stephanie Dostie; pg 48 – Shawn Dostie
Vito and His Daughter, Ariel: pg 49 – USMC
David and August: pg 54 – August Cabrera
Steven and Elizabeth: pg 57 – Free Pixabay Photo
Kevin and Theresa: pg 59 – Photographer Unknown; pg 64 – Theresa Morehead
A Message from Paul/Grandpa: pg 67 – Photographer Unknown
Joseph and Angie: pg 69 – Angela Boyd
James and Sarah: pg 74 & pg 77 – Photographer Unknown
Addison and His Granddaughter, Lila: pg 79 - Free Pixabay Photo
David and His Mother, Michelle: pg 83 – Michelle DeFord
Firefighter Michael and His Mother, Nancy: pg 84 – FDNY
Danial and Melany: pg 91 – Photographer Unknown
Michael and Jessica: pg 92 – Photographer Unknown; pg 95 – Jessica Braden Rogers
James and Lisa: pg 97 – Lisa Alvarez; pg 99 – L. Alvarez & Elegant Occasions
Hero of 9/11: pg 101 – Free Pixabay Photo
Joseph and Ashley: pg 103 – Photographer Unknown; pg 107 – Kevin Lawson
William and Maria: pg 108 & pg 110 – Maria Bonner
Shawn and Carrie: pg 113 – Shawn Reilly (1st picture) & Carrie Reilly (2nd picture)
Jason and Jennifer: pg 115 – Brent Hodges
David and Erin: pg 120 & pg 125 – Erin Yaggy

Foreword

By the Reverend Bill McDonald, Chaplain

For those who have lost loved ones in any war or in a cruel terrorist attack like 9/11, those losses take a huge piece of their heart and soul. That "long black cloud" Bob Dylan sings about does come down with its continuing veil of grief and sorrow. That is why stories such as those shared within this book become so powerful and important. They give those who have little hope for joy some inspiration and meaning. It reminds us all that life does not end with our worldly death. The stories within show that some can still *see* and *sense* that their loved ones continue to love and exist in another place; some may call this place heaven. They first begin to believe and then they *know* that those loved ones are still very much here with us even if invisible to human eyes or touch.

That long black cloud can be lifted and the darkness can be illuminated through our connections with our departed ones. Contacts through various mystical and spiritual encounters and feelings sometimes speak very loudly and clearly to the heart. They get our attention in various ways that make us realize they are indeed sending us a personal message. We know when they are real by how it makes us feel.

Never, ever, doubt the power of love to cross over and embrace us any time or any place. All I have found in my own life experiences verifies this to be the truth, time and time again.

I have had my own share of mystical experiences, which I have written about over the years in many books, but I get the greatest joy seeing how pure love can reunite us with those we have lost. It seems that death is not that vast dark undiscovered final frontier that we sometimes wrongly fear. Life and consciousness do go on and never cease. This I fully believe and *know* for a *fact!* I base this on my own near-death experiences and my own journeys on "the other side."

This book appears to many to take on a sad subject, but it actually opens up *"heaven's door"* just enough to give us the greatest hope and faith. I am honored to add a few words to this wonderfully inspired book. What the author sets out to do comes across totally as a pure act of love, which will add positive energy to the world.

[i]

This book is a sacred place for the memories of those who have contributed, but it is also an altar of hope that *heaven's door* is not really closed to those who love!

Preface

Baby, It's You

"*It's not the way you smile
That touched my heart
It's not the way you kiss
That tears me apart*"

—Burt Bacharach

The stories in this book come from survivors of people who died defending their country, both in the military and as civilians during disaster. They are love stories from the women and men who loved them—wives, relatives, and friends. And they are stories about how the survivors received messages from the deceased. Some are stories of war; some are about heroes of the World Trade Center tragedy on September 11, 2001.

The knock at the door brings the message that brides or mothers and fathers will always hear in their heads. The heart races at a speed no one wants to remember—starting from the moment they see casualty officers walk up the driveway to the moment they leave. Sometimes it isn't a knock at the door, but a suicide that changes lives too soon.

It is from that moment on for some that the love messages begin to unfold. They begin in any number of ways. "Their song" is played on the radio. A dream wraps around their love in circles. A smell recalls a special moment. A seemingly unending kiss sends shivers of what is to come. Perhaps it's a penny that miraculously appears in places no one could have left it.

It doesn't matter what the connection; all that matters is the loved one is gone from here, from how we knew them. Yet, they come to us in a different way.

Many of the widows, mothers, and soldiers in this book could not wait to tell their connections. These are beautiful stories from those who hold grief but move ahead each day, each hour, and each moment. They kiss their babies; they feed their families; they laugh on Facebook; and they share pictures of their memories.

It is all good, all bad, all ugly. It is life and death and the knowingness that the departed are still with us always and that love never dies. It is the smiles and kisses imprinted in our brains and hearts forever, the song or the dance that keeps us celebrating the memories. Cycles continue amid the chaos of life, with new marriages, new grandbabies, new puppies, and new messages.

Prayer and devotion guided many of these soldiers, now and before. Love is the tie that has no boundaries. It always connects forever and a day.

"Don't leave me alone,
Come on home
Baby, It's You."

—Shirelles

Till Death Do Us Not Part

Familiar songs continue to play from hearts that are always connected.

Pennies, feathers, heart shapes from nowhere, dreams that are waking.

Your message comes in the morning, in the night, time stops

"To have and to hold you from this day forward,

For richer, for poorer, in sickness and in health,

To love and to cherish from this day forward

Until death do us part."

Until death do us not part.

—Maureen McGill

Introduction

Just Like Romeo and Juliet

"Ah, all right now, I'm speculatin'
Wonder what tomorrow's really gonna bring ..."

—The Reflections

We met ...

... in the laundry room in college. He carried my underwear to my dorm room.

... in high school at a wrestling tournament.

... through my cousin.

... at Walmart where we worked.

... at a country bar on a Thursday night.

... at a nightclub on the dance floor.

... at a costume party with mask and a hat.

... on Instant Messenger. I was seventeen; he was nineteen.

... through his best friend Jeremy.

... in grade school when we played on the playground.

... on Facebook, and were married after one month of dating, at the pawn shop.

... on a blind date.

... on New Year's Eve.

... in the convertible when I stopped for a red light and he pulled up next to me.

... at Burger King where we worked at age sixteen.

... on a website called "Hot or Not," where we exchanged photos.

... when he was a football player and I was a cheerleader.

Baby, It's You

We meet now ...

... in my dreams.

... in the hallway when I smell him.

... in bed when I feel his skin touch mine.

... when I see his silhouette, his shoulders, his head, and how he held out his arms like he was holding a blanket.

... when the song comes on the radio at the restaurant, at church, or in an elevator.

... when I find pennies on the ground or in the weirdest places.

... when the basketball bounces on the court and no one's there.

... when I see him staring at me from the waist up when I am in bed.

... when I find the Dutch key ring in the middle of the desert, from him.

... when I meet the police officer who is wearing your memory bracelet.

... when I hear your voice saying, "My son."

... when the kids see you standing in uniform on the porch.

... when I find the heart-shaped sticker on a leaf.

... when the digital frame stops for no reason at your photo.

... when he comes to me in my dream with a message.

... when I hear his voice singing his favorite song.

Love Never Dies

It is only the body we cannot hold.

New breath follows us in dreams, visions,

waking magical moments that feel very real.

Songs fuel our hearts and dance in our memories.

That imprint never leaves.

It is all good, all bad, all ugly and

All beautiful. It is everlasting love.

—Maureen McGill

An American Soldier

(Sgt. Patrick McCaffrey, as told by his mother, Nadia, and wife, Silvia)

*"...if dying's asked of me,
I'll bear that cross with honor."*

—Toby Keith

My son Patrick and his wife of four years, Silvia, are the parents of two beautiful children, Junior and Janessa. I was visiting Silvia and Patrick one day and driving my old beat-up van. Checking my vehicle, Patrick had a displeased look on his face. He left the house with my van, came back and handed me a set of keys, saying only, "Mom, this is your car now."

"But that is your SUV-Yukon. Where is my van?"

Patrick's response: "I gave it away!"

"Aaaah!" My face dropped.

That was my son. He was managing two collision repair shops in California when the 9/11 terrorists attacked the world. His heart was moved to make a difference in his life. He enlisted as a volunteer in the National Guard, and by 2004 he was fighting in Iraq.

I knew in my heart as his mother that he would never return from the war. On the night before Patrick's deployment to Iraq, he and his little daughter Janessa, age two, were sitting in the master bedroom watching the *Lion King* movie, her favorite. She watched the Disney feature on average five times daily. I listened to their voices, thinking sadly that their family time was coming to an end.

At the part in the *Lion King* when Mufasa is killed in an ambush, betrayed by his brother, Janessa grabbed onto her father so hard she made a knot of her little fingers around Patrick's neck, near tears, telling him, "Daddy, that's you, Daddy, in war, dying!"

I cringed every time she said that. Patrick ran to me in the kitchen where Silvia and I were cooking dinner. His face was flushed. "Mom, do you know what Janessa just told me? I'm not coming back, am I, Mom?"

"Of course, you are. She is just a baby, sweetheart; she doesn't know."

But now I ask myself, did Janessa have knowledge of her daddy's fate? After Patrick left home that day, he was never to walk in the door again. It became a tradition for Janessa and me to watch the *Lion King* on a daily basis. Every time the film reached the death of the lion, Janessa curled up close to me and kept repeating, "Grandma, that's my daddy, that's my daddy!"

During Patrick's stay in Iraq, he became disillusioned with the mission and wrote this to me. He was overwhelmed with the hatred toward Europeans and Americans. Patrick was determined to be a good soldier. He wrote to me in an e-mail that he gave food and water to the children of the war, even though he was ordered not to give out anything. Those children reminded him of his own loving son and daughter.

Patrick's life was taken suddenly on June 22, 2004, after serving for three years. There was controversy over his death, the Pentagon stating he was killed in *conventional ambush*. I pursued the truth with national attention in the press and television news. It was revealed and later confirmed that Patrick was on a patrol with Iraqi Security Forces and the Platoon's LT when two soldiers were killed. Initially thought to be Iraqi insurgents in an ambush near Balad, Iraq, it was later revealed the soldiers were murdered by an Iraqi guardsman patrolling alongside my son, a man that Patrick was training. The third gunman drove up to the vehicle in a van and fired at the soldiers. It was a complete ambush. Patrick, a hero, was awarded a Bronze Star and Purple Heart.

Patrick's wife received the dreaded knock on the door from soldiers bearing the news. Silvia shouted to God, "Why did you take him? Why did you do this?"

I said, "God knows why; God will show you. You must rest now."

Silvia told me, "I went to our bedroom and closed my eyes; it was a kind of waking/sleeping vision. I saw Patrick in his uniform, the sun shining, a beautiful day. He was walking across this mountain and a group of marines were there to greet him, welcoming him with open arms."

Oh you went home, Patrick. It was clear you are home. I felt at peace; he was home.

For me it was a long and tedious battle to find the truth about his death, but I did it, gaining international coverage and recognition for my efforts. I now dedicate my life to service and have created a foundation for veterans—the Patrick McCaffrey Foundation. I am making a vision come true, providing housing and food for veterans. It is a sacred path of healing.

It was a hot California day when the family gathered back at the house after Patrick's funeral. My granddaughter, Janessa, was in the backyard playing with her dog Lucky near the lemon tree. She came running in the house to me and threw her arms around my legs.

"Daddy's here! Daddy's here!"

I went out to the backyard. On the asphalt I could see a vague image or energy, a filmy fog lifting from the surface. It was exactly where my granddaughter had seen Patrick. I could only see a vague image, but I knew it was him. We knew he was there, without any doubt.

Patrick's son, Junior, and his dad had often watched their favorite movie together, *Black Hawk Down*.

"We've watched that movie a hundred times together," Junior told another veteran when he went to visit his dad's gravesite.

The symbol of a rose became a sign for us from Patrick.

I remember three days after his death, a group of family and friends were at Patrick's house in Tracey, California. The house was packed with bouquets of flowers. We all crowded around the computer, watching a series of digital photos that soldier friends of Patrick had sent us from Iraq.

[3]

One of the photos was taken forty-five minutes before he was killed. Patrick is giving out food and vitamins to young children. He is sitting on the Humvee, and Iraqi children have just handed him a bouquet of white flowers. White roses appear as a symbol of purity and martyrdom, of the straight path and the paradise that awaits those martyred in God's cause in Islamic culture.

The digital picture frame stopped on the photo of Patrick in the Humvee with the white roses the children had given him. Out of nowhere, the roses in the bouquets disappeared and the overwhelming sweet fragrance of rose scent filled the entire room. The room instantly became quiet. During this moment of stillness we all stared at each other and began to cry. Silvia sweetly said, "Mom, it is Patrick, he is here with us now."

Silvia had another visit from Patrick, about six months later in a dream. "Patrick was dressed in all white, and looked very young. I said to him, 'Can you hold me, baby?' He answered, 'Okay, I will hold you.' I fell deep asleep in the dream, and when I woke, I could smell Patrick's cologne in the bedroom. I know it was him. It was to be the last dream for a long time from him."

I had another visit from Patrick in 2010, six years after Patrick's death. I was sleeping and woke from a dream that seemed real, not like any other dream I had of Patrick. He came to me dressed in his military uniform and I said, "My son, my son."

The hair on my arms stood up, it felt so real. I woke up immediately, feeling moved to speak with my grandson, Patrick's son.

"I'm fine, Grandma," he said. "Everything is a-ok!" The dream repeated two more times, Patrick always appearing in his army uniform.

The last message came on June 22, 2013, the anniversary of his death. "My son, my son."

This time I called Silvia, my daughter-in-law. "Is everything okay with your son?"

"Yes, everything is okay. Everything is fine."

After the third dream, I received a phone call. The young man was very upset on the line, crying and crying. "You probably don't want to see me now," he said. "My name is Florentino. My mother told me Patrick is my father, and he is dead now."

"Who is your mother?"

"Monique; they dated in high school."

You see, Patrick and Monique were dating in high school and they broke up suddenly. I remember Patrick telling me, "Oh, Mom, we broke up and Monique is moving away."

He never knew about the child.

DNA tests confirmed this was Patrick's son, and I brought the families together for a loving reunion. I knew this was a message from Patrick to prepare me for the call.

Silvia, Patrick's wife, did not have any dreams of Patrick soon after his death. It was quite sometime later when Silvia feels she had a visitation dream from him, one that felt so real.

"Our son Junior had signed up for the marines in the spring of 2014. I was on edge, and so was his grandmother Nadia, who was so nervous for Junior to be walking in the footsteps of his father. It was the night before Junior left for boot camp when I fell asleep and had this dream."

Patrick was sitting on a beach chair and he looked younger. Our daughter Janessa was playing on the beach.

Patrick said, "Our son left for boot camp, and everything will be fine, baby."

"Really," I said.

"Be supportive, and tell Mom to be supportive."

"Oh, babe," I said.

"He is strong. He is strong," he told me.

"I want to give you a hug," I said.

"You can't, baby."

Silvia said, "I woke up and thanked the Lord for this visit. I had a feeling Junior is fine now, not to worry. The last dream I had about Patrick was recently."

"Can you kiss me, baby?" I asked.

"No, I can't kiss you, baby," he said.

I was in the desert, and it was very sunny, but not that warm. Janessa and Junior were with me and I said to the kids, "Do you want to see Daddy? Okay, we are going to see Daddy."

I was wearing a white dress, and I had both of the kids dressed up in white, Junior in a white shirt and shorts, and Janessa in white dress, but no shoes or sandals. We were walking arm in arm, and we could see Patrick in the distance also dressed in white running to meet us. We started running to meet him. I heard him say to me, "Thank you, baby, for bringing my little princess and my junior to meet me. Take care of them."

"I promise, I will, baby."

"I know you will, baby."

"Don't worry about Junior; he will be fine!"

"I felt so comforted by this dream," Silvia said.

One of Patrick's best friends and a brother in arms, Thomas McGuire, had a strange experience and has no doubt this came from Patrick on the other side. Tom is pretty shy. A group from their unit met at the armory in Petaluma, California, shortly after Patrick died. They all loved to play basketball, and Patrick was always the lively one, always joking and yelling. So, the pals gathered and played.

Tom said, "We were taking a break and all of a sudden the ball was self-acting! It was literally bouncing on its own on the court. 'Cut it out, Patrick,' I shouted, and the ball stopped. We knew it was him."

"'Cause freedom don't come free.
I'm an American soldier, an American."

—Toby Keith

Patrick and His Mother, Nadia

By the Reverend Bill McDonald, adapted for this book

(Sgt. Patrick McCaffrey and his mother, Nadia McCaffrey)

[NOTE: Bill shared this story with me about how the signs continued for Nadia McCaffrey, Gold Star mother of Patrick McCaffrey, and for himself. Reverend Bill is a Vietnam veteran, now a chaplain and healer who is known in the world for his gift of spirituality and wise work with veterans. Bill shared the song "Somewhere Over the Rainbow" (by Harold Arlen and Yip Harburg) as a memory of this story for this book. —MM]

A short time after I wrote my first book, *A Spiritual Warrior's Journey,* I got an odd phone call in the middle of the night from a publisher who owned a small book publishing company in Arkansas. He was calling me around Christmastime, excited about having read my book and shared his feelings about it. He went on about how he could identify with lots of the stuff I had written in the book and how he was emotionally moved reading it. I was on the phone patiently waiting for him to say something like *"We want to publish all your next books with us!"* But, that was not why he was calling.

After discussing various stories in my book with me and talking for perhaps an hour, he finally got around to telling me about a woman he knew that I just had to meet. She lived not too far from where I lived in the big central valley of California. She was one of those people who had had an NDE (near-death experience) and was lecturing around the country. He felt that she and I needed to meet. He gave me some contact information on this woman and then we hung up. I wasn't sure why I needed to meet her, but the conversation and circumstances were so odd that I figured there must be some good reason.

Weeks later, I finally got around to getting in touch with her at her home in Tracy, California. Her name was Nadia McCaffrey. She was about my age and was a naturalized American citizen. She grew up in France and had married an American GI and come to the USA.

She had one son who had been killed recently in the war on terrorism. I agreed to meet her. She told me she was going to be in Stockton, not too far from my home, and would be doing a press conference there with a small group who were protesting the war.

I was not very keen about protesting any cause, let alone this war, but I did show up and found her facing several different TV cameras. They were from stations all across northern California, including the San Francisco Bay area. She was wearing an all-black outfit. Her blond hair contrasted rather well with the dark clothing. She seemed to be very comfortable in front of the press, talking with a French accent. I stood off to the side, slightly off camera, watching it all while trying not to get in the way.

Then my cell phone went off, right in the middle of one of her live interviews. I had a very distinct phone ring for calls from my ex-daughter-in-law, Syd—her voice shouting out to answer the phone. There, in the middle of a very serious live interview, my phone started making very loud sounds of a woman shouting. To make matters worse, it was in my pocket, and it took forever to get it out. Everyone stopped to look at me—so much for ruining a live television news broadcast.

Gone as well was trying to keep a low profile at Nadia's press conference. My cover was blown. I was noticed by everyone there and heard by the TV audience! That was the first time we met, but not the last time. This all blossomed into a great working relationship. It eventually led to us partnering with her nonprofit organization, which helps PTSD veterans deal with returning home from the war. I became the organization's official chaplain and spiritual advisor. She became my good friend.

Her life was truly an inspirational story. She told me about her two experiences with death—one from a bite from a poisonous wasp, which happened to her as a young girl living on a farm in France. She was in a coma for a long time and had one of those typical NDE events where you pass over into the light. She felt so loved she didn't wish to come back to her life in the physical body.

Her next NDE was from her own hand as she tried to end her life. She had remembered how wonderful and loving it was on the other side. I'm glossing over many details in this brief account of her younger life, but she always felt that she was still in this life for a much greater purpose. She always felt she had a mission; now at this stage of her life, after the death of her son, she was definitely on a mission. She was trying to help other young veterans get their lives back together again through the foundation she formed.

Nadia was truly being a mother-like figure for these veterans. She had a heart of gold and their worries and problems were hers as she labored all over the country and the world for their cause. She was getting old houses and farm property to use as places where these young men and women could get their feet back on the ground after the war. Some of them might need to stay only a few weeks, while others may need six months or longer to get themselves readjusted. These were planned as "spiritual retreats," but without all the formal religious overtones. In other words, spiritual-based living that was not religious. Anyway, that was the way I saw the effort.

She had managed to get six houses in upstate New York and a piece of property along the Russian River in northern California. At the time of this writing, she was looking to raise enough money to buy an old abandoned college campus in Minnesota. It took hard work to raise both the awareness and funding. She was always off across the country speaking and lobbying for her troops. One such speaking engagement took her to the far reaches of northern California along the coast in Humboldt County. She was going to drive up there alone, so I volunteered to go with her for safety and assistance.

The drive north was more than eight hours long, giving us a long conversation together. I learned all kinds of interesting things about her life and that of her son Patrick. She told me about how a big white owl had appeared in her backyard in the daytime on the anniversary of the day her son was killed, like he was communicating with her. She told me about all kinds of supernatural events surrounding his death and how she found out. I could sense we were cut of the same kind of spiritual cloth. She was a mystic and a powerful soul.

I told her a bunch of my own owl stories. I related to her how they always appeared to me as a spiritual messenger. I even had an owl fly directly in front of my truck windshield to lead me down a curvy mountain road at night. I've had them perch in my backyard in broad daylight. I also related the story of having seen two of them having sex in a church bell tower during the memorial service of a good friend, which let me know that life was going on and that my friend was fine. Sometimes the sightings come when I am talking about them, as what transpired at the Hidden Valley Men's Ashram, run by the Self-Realization Fellowship.

On that occasion, I was walking with a fellow Vietnam veteran in the back woods of the ashram telling him how owls were my symbol and how, whenever I needed encouragement or a spiritual boost in energy, they showed up in my life.

The man I was talking to interrupted my story by saying, "Do you mean owls like that?"

There, just a few yards from us, sitting on a large boulder in the bright afternoon sunshine, was just such an owl. He looked directly at the both of us. It was perfect timing, and my friend was silent in respect of the situation. Those owl's eyes lovingly watched us both until we walked away.

I finally ended my conversation, saying something about how people I relate to well have had some kind of an owl experience with me or on their own. I told her that sometimes I go into people's homes and discover they have a large collection of owl statues, or pictures of owls, or artwork depicting them. I said it is uncanny how often this happens.

When we reached our destination, we got out of the car and found the keys left by the woman who owned the house. She was away at work, but had left the place for us to spend the night. When we went inside, we saw owl things all over her home. Even the kitchen towel had owl images on it. We shook our heads and smiled. It felt like the right place to spend the weekend.

I found myself very ill that night when the time came for us to deliver a speech to a group raising money for a veteran project. I stayed on the sofa and, for the first time in my life, missed a speaking engagement. Normally, I would go, come hell or high water, but I was violently ill and throwing up. I never moved off the sofa until the next morning.

Both Nadia and our host had been at the veterans' event the night before and were looking for the blown-up photos of Patrick, Nadia's son, she had brought on the trip. She takes these to some of these veterans' events to talk about her son. She was upset, afraid she had lost them, or had left them behind at the event. She was beside herself with grief. The photos meant a lot to her, especially since this morning was her son's birthday.

She and the other woman had gone throughout the entire house and car looking for them, all to no avail. They sat despondent in the kitchen and told me about how they lost them. Nadia was getting more upset. I suggested they look again. They made another sweep around the house. When Nadia went into the bedroom, where she had looked twice already, she saw the photos sitting on the floor next to the bed. They were not there earlier when she had spent several minutes looking for them. She came out of the bedroom feeling that it must have been divinely connected somehow with her son, since this was his birthday.

I suggested that we do a little prayer ceremony for her son in the backyard of this house. There was a small water fountain and lots of open space. We set up the photos next to the fountain, and the three of us gathered to pray for her son Patrick. Just as soon as we stopped praying, the local church bells began to ring. They were ringing loudly, and it added to our offerings. Then I said a few words. As we closed the short service, Patrick's photos fell over, face down, onto the cement patio. Then the winds picked up and made all of the wind chimes in the yard begin to beat out their music. It was a wonderful spiritual moment. We listened and watched in awe at the magic unfolding around us.

As suddenly as it had begun, the wind subsided. It became totally silent. Not even the birds were singing. We picked up the photos and went inside the house, feeling that Patrick had found a way to send his love to his mother from the other side. It certainly made her feel wonderful.

"If happy little bluebirds fly
Beyond the rainbow,
Why oh why can't I?"

—Harold Arlen and E. Y. Harburg

No one can deceive you with owl medicine in the Native American
traditions, no matter how they try to disguise or hide it from you.
The truth always brings enlightenment!

—Medicine Cards by Jamie Sams

Robert and Ally

(Pfc. Robert Wheatley, as told by his wife, Ally)

"I'm here without you, baby
But you're still on my lonely mind"

—Three Doors Down

We were introduced by mutual friends in 2007. Pfc. Robert Wheatley was stationed at Fort Lewis, Washington, and had returned home from a one-year deployment to Iraq to care for his ailing mother. He was to return to Iraq in September for his second tour.

Ours was a different courtship; we became friends by texting each other. Our first date was walking together at Veterans Park in Porterville, California. We talked and laughed the entire time. As I drove out of the park, he was in the car behind, texting me, "When will I see you again?"

"Tonight!" I responded.

We were inseparable after that. Within two months, he moved in with my children and me, and in eight months we were married. It was a very short marriage.

That morning in May I had a feeling he had left me. He had left home for Fort Lewis. I can't describe the feeling except I knew he was gone. I started to panic when he didn't return at the usual time, so I began calling friends, when soldiers came to the door to deliver the message. Four months after we married, in May 2009, *Pfc. Robert Wheatley US ARMY died in a stateside accident.* He had served a year-long tour in Iraq, but died in May before he was to begin his second tour in September.

He died in a rafting accident after field training on the Nisqually River. His brigade was preparing for its second deployment to Iraq. They got hung up on a log jam, the rafts overturned, and his body was missing for sixteen days.

As a couple, we were connected. Robert always woke early, partly to be ready for PT (physical training); I am not a morning person at all. He was always bubbly in the mornings, happily calling to me, "Come on, baby, wake up." He wanted me up and awake with him.

I had four kids when I married Robert, and he took them on as his own. My children called him *Daddy*, and their biological father, *Dad*.

After he died, I often woke up with a start at 4 a.m. for no reason. I'd be wide awake, sitting right up. I could feel Robert's presence. I feel him often. I used to sleep in his armpits. Every once in a while I smell his deodorant, *Degree*. I often get a whiff of that specific fragrance—a clean, neutral scent with subtle citrus notes, very distinctive.

He used to wrap around me at night, and I can feel him sometimes now, when I am about to drift off to sleep. He is right there, and I feel a slight squeeze. Sometimes, I am sitting in a chair and I can feel his touch or smell him. I know it is him. Occasionally, I will hear our song, "I'm Here Without You," by Three Doors Down, and know it is Robert.

A few years after his death, I worked up the courage to meet someone for a date. Robert was a jealous guy, always very jealous if I even looked at anyone else. I was driving on a city street when out of the blue, that song, our song, came on the radio. I had to turn the car around. I knew I didn't have his permission to see anyone else yet, and somehow I could not meet this new fellow. It felt almost dangerous to meet this man. I knew it was Robert! I like to think I was being protected.

The time we felt the most connected in our relationship was the first time he said *I love you.* It was magic; I cannot explain it; we really connected with "I love you." I hear the whisper of his voice as clear as a bell sometimes. I know it is him. He is with me.

My biggest *wink* was two years after he passed. I had booked a big hotel for the kids and me. Robert and I had stayed at the hotel in the past, and this time we were assigned the exact room number as the one Robert and I shared on our first vacation together! He was with us.

Robert always tried to make me laugh. A framed photo of him sits in the living room. I took a photograph of it one day and found all these orbs, which appeared all over the photo. They were like circular whirlwinds all over the room. I have no doubt it was him. It is so comforting to me to know he is here always. I can't wait to see him when that happens. When I take pictures of the kids, I see the orbs too, and I feel it is Robert always with them. This year has been a healing year for me. Finally, I can jump in the water again. I know he is with us.

"But all the miles that separate
Disappear now when I am dreaming of your face."
—Three Doors Down

Alan and Amber

(Spc. Alan J. Younger, as told by his wife, Amber)

"The moment I wake up ...
I say a little prayer for you."

—Hal David

We met each other when we both were in the service. I was in training to be a combat medic. We connected quickly and soon were pregnant with our little girl Mareska. This began a challenging journey; I was twenty-one and he was twenty. I had to leave the National Guard because of a hardship with little Mareska.

We waited to get married for a couple of years, deciding to be close friends before we officially tied the knot. We had a simple courthouse wedding and a beautiful trip to Jackson Hole, Wyoming, for a delayed honeymoon, with whitewater rafting and fun times.

Alan was a tanker in Bagdad. He had a history of mental instability. I pleaded with him to get therapy, but he wouldn't consent to it. Two days before our fourth anniversary (our daughter was seven), Alan took his life in front of me. He had attempted suicide multiple times in his life. I don't think it was only the deployments; he had a history of mental instability before that, including deep depression. He would often mask it or outsmart the illness so no one would know. Now, I have the pain of those final moments, physically manifesting the pain of that final second.

We didn't have a song, but one song stuck with me, Aretha Franklin's version of "I Say a Little Prayer for You." Before Alan's death,

I would go through my day, thinking of him, but not as a lovesick girl. It was only a song that resonated for us.

I have dreams, mostly nightmares, about our connection together and, of course, all the memories of his final day. One dream I had about Alan had me walking into a hospital where he was on life support. In the dream, the doctors says, "Alan is in a medically induced coma, and we are going to wake him up."

"Don't wake him up; don't bring him back," I shout.

"He doesn't want that; he doesn't want to be there." They woke him up from the coma, and Alan pulled out the IVs and yelled at the doctors, angry that they woke him up.

"He doesn't want to be here," they are saying. "We are so sorry," the docs shouted.

A special experience that I know was him reaching out to me with a message on January 2014, about five months after he died. I was going through the emotions and grief of this horrific experience, ready to run away. I bought a plane ticket to Seattle to visit a friend and boarded the plane. Each seat had those little movie screens on the headrest in front of you, to watch films during the flight.

Midway through the flight all the power to the movies went down and a little cartoon penguin came on the screen. I unbuckled my seat belt and saw the penguins projected on everyone's screen; everyone was talking and laughing about it. *What is going on?* Well, I remembered, Alan's favorite animal was the penguin. He liked to play video penguins and doodle with our daughter—little penguins. *Why is there a penguin?* As I looked at all these penguins, I thought, then shouted out loud: "Really, Alan? Really? Really, Al?"

Five minutes later, the power returned and the penguin comes out with, "Do you really have to be in everyone's face?"

I have a fear of flying, so when I realized it was a penguin message, I knew it was Alan. I thought maybe we were going to crash. That was Alan, messing with the cartoons to make me laugh!

Penguins share the spiritual animal energies of duty, survival, and epic journey. It is written that the penguin symbolizes animal magic, clairsentience, and imagination! No doubt Alan was there!

I got another sign from Alan. On September 27, 2014, I participated in a suicide prevention fundraiser. It's called the "Out of the Darkness" walk and it's sponsored by the American Foundation for Suicide Prevention. I participated in Alan's memory. Everyone who lost someone to suicide released a balloon with their loved one's name on it. I did one for Alan. About one hundred balloons were released.

Well, one night almost a month after the fundraiser and balloon release, my friend Sandy, who lives three miles from the park where we released the balloons, texted me a picture. She wrote, "My dog found this in my backyard for you." Alan's balloon had traveled to her house. It was deflated when the dog brought it to Sandy. It is marked with the tribute to "Alan Younger, 6-2-87–8-12-13" with the infinity symbol drawn on the balloon.

What makes it odder still is that the fundraiser was in a town I don't live in, and Sandy is the only person I know who lives there. His balloon traveled back to me through her. Alan wanted me to know he is with us.

Robert and Holly

(Fc2 Robert Campbell E5, as told by his wife, Holly)

*"...nothing, nothing can ever
Change this love I have for you."*

—Sam Cooke

Bobby and I met through mutual friends while we were both living in Hawaii in 2010. He was stationed there at the time. When I left after meeting him for the first time, he apparently told our mutual friend he was going to marry me. It was definitely love at first sight for both of us.

Within that first year, we married and found out we were pregnant with our first and only child, Mason. Our son was my husband's world from the moment we knew we were pregnant. Our song together was, "Nothing Can Change This Love," by Sam Cooke, no matter how many miles apart we became.

We were such homebodies together. We often canceled plans with friends just to stay home, lie on the couch, and watch our favorite shows together. Every Sunday we went to real estate open houses around the island and pretended we were living in that house. My husband wanted to invest in real estate so we would check out houses on the market, but we couldn't help imagining how we'd decorate each room, even if we couldn't afford some of the houses.

We moved to San Diego in January 2013 and loved exploring the city and finding new places together. He was on active duty at the time.

Unfortunately, on August 15, 2013, I had a doctor's appointment that would change our lives. My husband met me at the appointment after coming straight from work. He was late, which was odd, but he showed up. Bobby had decided to follow me and my son home, even though he knew very well how to get home from there. We suddenly were stopped in bumper-to-bumper traffic, and my husband couldn't stop in time. He rear-ended my car and sustained many injuries. An hour later, he was gone.

The doctors tried everything to save him, but his injuries were too severe. He was active duty at the time of the accident and was even wearing his uniform at the time.

FC2 Robert Campbell, an E5 on the USS *Russell*, was only twenty-three when he passed, two months away from his birthday. My son and I remember every second of that day as if it happened yesterday. Within a blink of an eye, our lives were forever changed.

We miss him more than I thought was humanly possible. Together, we honor his memory in every way we can. After he died, my son and I went to San Jose for the service. His family was going through photos and I found the cutest photo of my Bobby when he was nine years old. I absolutely fell in love with that photo and started calling him my sunflower. A couple days later at his service, an arrangement of sunflowers waited for us at the church with no name on it! We have no clue to this day where it came from. I have seen sunflowers ever since. Whether they were real flowers, prints on someone's dress, or a picture, they started to appear everywhere. I saw them a lot when I was with my friend, Monique, and now she sees them too. But the weird part is, she only sees them when she's thinking of me, or about to see me in person. If she sees a sunflower out of the blue, she will text or call me to see if I'm okay and 99 percent of the time, I'm not okay. I'll be having a really rough time.

Bobby knew I was never one to reach out to anybody when I'm having a tough time, so we both feel it's his way of reaching out for me and sending help when I need it most. This past fall, my son and I were getting pumpkins when we came upon a similar sunflower cutout just like the one my husband's picture was in. I dreaded getting the pumpkins to carve because it was always something Bobby wanted to do as a family. Seeing that sunflower at the pumpkin patch was my sign from him that it was all okay, that he would still be there in spirit. He was showing me not to dread family traditions just because a piece of our family was missing.

I have seen my husband in a couple of dreams, but my biggest sign from him is finding bobby pins. I didn't catch on right away and was confused why I kept finding bobby pins, knowing I don't use them in my hair! Once I finally caught on, all I could do was laugh and thank my husband for showing me he was still around. The first time I found the bobby pins, I was sitting in my car. It was the car that was involved in the accident, and I just sat there crying, taking everything in while just sitting. That was our first family car and we had many memories in it.

I started rummaging around, cleaning out some garbage, when I found the first one in the backseat. My first honest reaction was to wonder what woman my husband had in *my* car, since I don't wear them! Within the next few days, I found more. A couple more in my car, one on the floor of my room, then one in my bed! That's when it hit me that it was my husband; things instantly clicked. I sat in bed giggling, with tears streaming down my face, thanking him for showing me. I had been begging him for a sign, and I was just oblivious at first.

That's when I started to pay attention to the little things. There isn't too much more I can say about the bobby pins. They just happen to pop up when I need them most. Whether I'm thinking of and missing Bobby or I'm going through a really hard time, there they are. My favorite is when I'm in a really bad mood, not happy at all, and everything seems to be getting to me. When I least expect it in a moment like that, I'll find a bobby pin. It puts everything in perspective for me and allows me to take a step back, breathe deeply, and realize that everything is going to be okay.

I have only had two dreams involving my husband since he passed. The first was just two nights after he died. We were walking between a huge building and a river, just walking, but he wasn't walking with me. He was in front of me, walking away. I couldn't see his face, but I knew it was him. There was someone walking next to him, but I still haven't figured out who it is. They're talking as if I'm not there, and Bobby keeps mentioning his little brother Justin. In an instant, it's over.

The other dream is amazing. It came to me while we were still in the process of making funeral arrangements. I was so on edge at that time; I kept saying I didn't like that my husband's body was alone and cold somewhere. He needed to be at his final resting place, but time seemed to drag. So the message from this dream was needed.

I had dreamed I was sitting on my couch in my living room and both of my casualty officers were sitting at the dining room table. They both looked at me and smiled and one said, "There's someone here who wants to see you."

A huge bright light came shining through the sliding glass door as it opened very gracefully, and in walks my husband. The description I've heard of the light, the loving feeling you get when you see heaven's light, is exactly what I felt in that moment. My husband glided through the door, staring right at me and smiling the biggest smile I've ever seen. Again, he didn't speak to me in the dream, but I got this overwhelming feeling knowing he was at peace. I woke up with tears of joy.

Our song doesn't come on the radio, but Sam Cooke's songs come on often. The Sunday after my husband died, I went out to breakfast with my son, my husband's uncle, and my sister-in-law. While sitting in Denny's, Sam Cooke's music started playing on the radio and I completely broke down. Again, just a couple days later, I picked my mom up from the airport and we had stopped at Ross to get shoes for the funeral, and another song by Sam Cooke came on! And this song was another of our favorites about having a party and being happy. It showed me that he was living it up in heaven and having a blast. I again broke down and probably looked so ridiculous, standing in Ross, holding shoes and crying. We both used to listen to the entire Sam Cooke album while showering at night. While we showered, he'd sing every song to me.

Cameron and Timi

(Cpl. Cameron P. Branum, as told by his wife, Timi)

"We're a dream come true,
suited perfectly for eternity."
—Kenny Chesney

We met each other in high school in 2006, when Cameron was a senior and I was a junior. Cameron was a laid-back fun-loving guy who loved to help anyone and everyone any chance he got. We went to different high schools, but both worked at the local grocery store. We became friends. Finally, he asked me out ... when I quit working there. He wouldn't date anybody he worked with. We had our first date in 2007; we went to the movie *Shooter*, probably the worst movie we had both ever seen. We laughed about that for years to come.

When Cameron enlisted in the US Marines, we didn't have much time together. We had only been together three or four months, and I felt if we can make it through boot camp, we can make it through anything. In the free times we could get together, we spent hours walking and sitting on the beach. We decided to get married on one of his leaves, and our wedding was a simple occasion—outdoors in May on a hot Oklahoma day. I wore a simple summer dress, and he wore plaid pants and a white button-up shirt.

He served as a rifleman with the 1st Fleet Antiterrorism Security Team Company based in Norfolk, Virginia, for two years. We didn't ever get a chance to honeymoon, but he made up for it once I moved out to Virginia, making every day a special day.

We have three sons; Cameron met two of them. Our oldest son, Gavyn, was born almost a year and half after we were married, two days before Christmas. Cameron was deployed to Afghanistan in 2011 for eight months. During that deployment, he loved to sing to me or send me verses from the Kenny Chesney song, "Me and You."

Our second son, Ayden, was born during that time. Ayden was two months old when I handed him over to his father upon his return from deployment. I will never forget the light in Cameron's eyes.

Cameron never got to meet his third son, Presley. He died in a stateside active duty motorcycle accident, two days after Christmas 2012. Presley was born three months to the day that Cameron died. I hold him as close to my heart as with the other boys, knowing the joy and love they represent to me.

I have received what I refer to as "winks" from Cameron from day one. The first wink happened the night of December 27, the day he died. I was lying in bed crying and crying, barely asleep, when I swear up and down I heard Cameron whisper, "I love you, baby girl."

I woke up looking for him because it sounded as if he were right there with me.

Another one came about a week after his funeral service. I was at his gravesite, weeping away because life seemed so horrible and not worth going on. It was very windy. Out of nowhere, a leaf blew into the opening of my jacket. I looked down at it and said, "What the he—?"

There was a little metal heart stuck on the leaf. I knew immediately it was a message from Cameron, and it lifted my spirits. What are the chances of finding a metal heart-shaped silver leaf stuck on a tree leaf right by his gravesite? I knew it was Cameron.

The third wink happened when I was once again at his graveside. I went there often during the months after his passing. That day was the first time I had taken our two young kids. Out of the corner of my eye, I saw something shiny on the ground. I tried hard to ignore it, but it kept catching my eye. I walked over to see what it was and found a little heart-shaped sticker.

The one that makes me cry the most happened when I finally got up the strength and courage to unpack his clothes from the boxes, which were sent to me by the movers. I was listening to Pandora on my phone, and the very first song that came on the list, which I had not programmed, was "Me and You" sung by Kenny Chesney. This has always been our song. Cameron not only sang it to me when he was deployed, he sang it to me whenever it came on the radio. I knew it was Cameron again.

Hearing the song on the radio made me cry even more. I sank to my knees bawling. While it made me miss him and cry, I know he was right there with me, letting me know he loves me and that he knows I miss him.

"I hear you laughin' in the rain.
I still can't believe you're gone."

—Kenny Chesney

John and Ann

(Pfc. John Judge, as told by his love, Ann)

[NOTE: Names have been changed to protect identities. —MM]

In 1967, "All You Need Is Love" was broadcast on AM stations around the world. "It was for love and bloody peace," John Lennon echoed. The Associations, the Beatles, Frankie Valli, and Petula Clark sang the songs of that time that pulled heart strings and peace strings.

I attended high school in northern California. John Judge was a classmate, tall, athletic, part Native American, with warm brown eyes and an outgoing personality. I had long beautiful flowing hair, was a dancer full of smiles. We both excelled in school and fell for each other. He was the love of my life. It was a mature, intimate relationship, and a connection way beyond our years. We always felt like old souls.

We dated seriously from our sophomore year to our senior year. We both had plans to attend college, and questions arose whether or not to continue our romance. He was on edge with the draft happening for Vietnam; after seeing an advertisement about being "a buddy in the marines," he decided to sign up. Before he signed the final papers he asked me to tie the knot.

"At long last love has arrived; you're too good to be true": Frankie Valli's lyrics echoed as a truth.

I couldn't marry then; I had plans to finish college, goals to work in the financial sector. I felt I was too young to settle into the commitment of marriage. He got upset with me and struggled with my decision. Our communication broke down when he went to boot camp and became Pfc. John Judge at age nineteen.

He wasn't in Vietnam more than two weeks when his family got word he had stepped on a land mine and perished. I received the news at college through a friend, six months after the funeral.

Five years after his passing, I began to feel an extremely strong sense of his presence. I'd have waking visions where I would see a cameo headshot of him, his beautiful skin and radiant smile, as if no time had passed—just as I remember him at age eighteen. He appeared frequently, usually at the time I was taking a break, being quiet, sitting in stillness, when he would come for a visit. He was always smiling, always radiant, always the same, a strong youthful vibration.

Recently, thirty-five years since his passing, I received a special, direct message from John. I had been working on the fortieth class reunion and had an interest in genealogy. I researched all the classmates who had died and was compiling a memorial list. I seemed to be guided to answers to why they died so young. I found myself digging into the causes of their death. I felt an obligation to memorialize these classmates for the reunion. We dedicated a special table at the reunion to those who had died since high school.

It was at this time when I received a kind of confirmation of John's presence. A friend of mine opened a coffee shop in a Northwest harbor town where I was living. One Saturday morning I walked in to buy a coffee and saw a gentleman sitting on a bench next to a small table.

The man spoke up, "Hello, my name is George, and I would like to speak with you." I realized he was a psychic. "I would love to do a reading for you. You are like a subway station, with people coming and going around you on the other side. You are so busy right now. I know you might not be into that, but I sense the presence of a past boyfriend around you, a male who died in Vietnam, someone you knew."

I was intrigued and felt he was authentic and consented to hear more.

"I see this guy around you that you were very involved with at one time in your life, and he died in Vietnam. He has a wonderful smile, and he wants you to know that he is here with you."

George continued to confirm many details about the presence of my lost love. "He wants to go with you and through you. He wants you to know he died of friendly fire ... repeat ... friendly fire, and you need to tell his family about that."

"I can't tell his family; it wouldn't serve any purpose for me to do that now."

I went to the reunion and stayed in the guest room of my brother's home. I was sleeping in my grandmother's carved bed. It was about that moment between waking and sleeping when I felt John's presence. I could see him from the chest up, touching me, the feeling strong and real, sweetness and gentleness moving through the dance of passionate love. It was so real I could feel him. I saw his smile and heard his words.

"Are you really making love, John, to an eighteen-year-old woman, or to the fifty-eight-year-old woman that I am now?" I asked.

"To both. Your spirit is all the same," his voice echoed. "Your spirit is the same, there is no difference."

It was like he was inserting the words into my mind as dialogue. John was with me, I have no doubts.

[NOTE: As Ann was telling this story, the Stones' song, "War, Children," echoed in the background with the plaintive words, "It's just a shot away ... just a kiss away." —MM]

David and Melinda

(Spc. David A. Wilkey, as told by his wife, Melinda)

"So take my hand and hold on tight
And we'll get there
Oh, we'll get there—this I swear."

—Nick Lachey

David and I lived across town from each other, and we began talking on Instant Messenger when I was seventeen and David was nineteen. Before he ever saw my house, he knew exactly how my room was arranged. Honestly, I was a little freaked out at first. I had a baby just over a year old, and I knew I couldn't play games.

We continued to chat online and finally decided to meet at a high school regional wrestling tournament. David had already graduated, and I was a junior who managed our school wrestling team. I felt nervous. When I walked through those doors to the gym, he stood with his back to me, blue shirt, jeans, and black dress shoes. Hair was gelled and spiked up a little in the front. He turned around at the perfect time as I walked through the door, and my nerves shot up.

I walked over to him and we introduced ourselves and found a seat in the bleachers behind my team. We talked and flirted a little throughout the whole meet. When it was time to go (January 2004 was very cold), we stood outside in the blistering cold for about an hour talking. He didn't wear a coat, and he finally walked me over to my grandma's van.

I stepped in and leaned forward on the steering wheel looking up into his baby blues. As I sat staring into his eyes, he quickly leaned in and kissed me. After kissing me, he quickly apologized. I assured him it was okay, and we said our goodbyes.

We became a couple in early February 2004 and were married in December 2005. Our wedding was a quick one because we were about to become parents to a baby boy at any moment.

He was gone a lot of the first year, on duty with the army, and we never made it to the second-year anniversary.

One memorable moment was the mud fight we had. David, my sister, my two boys, and I began flinging mud at each other and wrestling in the mud and the kiddie pool. My sister and I also covered his truck in mud! We laughed a lot.

David did not meet our second child, a daughter; I was five months pregnant when he was killed. Army specialist David A. Wilkey, age twenty-two, died when a roadside bomb blew up near his unit in Baghdad. He was riding in a Humvee.

We found connections with such songs as "Cheatin'" by Teri Evans and "This I Swear" by Nick Lachey. The Lachey song was played at our wedding. Two other songs, which have sentimental value now, are "American Soldier" by Toby Keith. We played this one at the memorial ceremony at Fort Riley. One of his NCOs said that David would walk around singing "American Soldier" all the time.

The other song he sang was "If You're Reading This," a song written by Tim McGraw and dedicated to soldiers who have died. The song is written in the form of a letter to the family of a soldier who had died, to be sent to them upon dying. The timing of David singing that song was right before he died. David didn't know we were having a baby girl. We didn't know until August or September. She was born on her due date, October 7, 2007. Every time I hear the song, "If You're Reading This," it makes me cry thinking about him and the relationship the baby will never have with her father.

We were flown in from Fort Riley, Kansas, to the upper peninsula of Michigan, where he was buried in the Spalding/Powers Cemetery, in his hometown. His heart was always in Michigan. He eventually wanted all of us to move up there.

Late on the night after we laid my husband to rest, we went back to the hotel to pack up. While packing, my grandmother bent down, then she stood back up holding white male tighties! (male underpants) in her hands. It was the same brand David wore.

"Ewww," my grandmother said as she tossed the pants at me! The lights in the room immediately started flickering on and off. "All right, David, we know you're here," my grandmother said emphatically. The lights immediately stopped flickering as soon as my grandmother shouted.

We knew he heard us when the lights stopped.

We were all females in the room. The beds had stoppers at the base, so it is unlikely the pants were left in the room by someone else. We asked the housekeeper in the morning if there was an electrical problem at the hotel or if they had complaints about the lights. She assured us there were no reports of light issues. The only personal belongings I had of David's were his dog tags, some pictures, and the rings he wore on the day of the incident. This was David playing a trick on us, no doubt!

I still get messages from him. I was having a bad day not long after his passing. I called out, "David, I need some guidance for strength, and a sign from you." I looked down on the ground and there was a dime, dated 1984, the year David was born. Messages continue. When I see dimes, I find them in multiples of threes, either for three kids, or three very important people I have lost in my life. My grandpa died, David died, and two years later, my boyfriend died—all within a short time.

When my daughter was in my womb, we decided to name her "Genesis Ane." But when I received David's notebook from his footlocker after he died, he had asked me to name her Alexa.

Messages come even to my daughter, six years later. A few weeks ago she told me, "I saw Daddy come through the wall."

"How do you know it's Daddy?" I asked.

"Because I have blue eyes just like Daddy!" She knows what he looks like because I have pictures everywhere.

There have been other messages from him. Whenever I begin to forget his smell, the wind blows, and I get a brief trace of him as if he passed by me. The smell I get from him is hard to describe. I remember getting up early in the morning when he was getting ready to go hunting, and he smelled like hunting gear. It's hard to describe the smell he had before he went hunting. And when he wasn't in hunting gear, he smelled of Cool Water Cologne. It's kind of like fresh linen hanging on a clothesline type of scent with a mixture of lavender, jasmine, musk, and sandalwood.

The most recent message came as we were visiting his gravesite in northern Michigan. I was about to go to sleep, and I had not cried for him in a while. That night I asked him to hold me after I got off the computer. I lay down and could feel him wrap his arms around me and hold me until I fell asleep.

It was the best night's sleep I had all weekend.

"I'll never let you down, my love."

—Nick Lachey

Kenney and Melissa

(MSG Kenney Wilson, as told by his wife, Melissa)

"...he'll always run
To sweet Melissa."

—Allman Brothers

MSG Kenney Bruce Wilson's best friend Jeremy was one of my closest friends. I had been super close to Jeremy and his wife, Stacy, for years. We met at Jeremy's going-away party. Kenney was handsome and strong, with the most beautiful smile. I was tall, thin, wearing my hair to my shoulders. Our connection was instant. We had our first date a week later and spent the entire weekend together just talking and getting to know each other. It was amazing like even holding hands we could feel the electricity.

I was going out with a group of guy friends to an event called the Dogwood Festival when Kenney called to see if I was available. I invited him out to the festival, but warned him I was with a group of guys, and at least half of them were gay. Kenney was a big Special Forces guy, so I thought he wouldn't come, but he said, "Great, I'll see you soon."

He hung out with us all night. Fun little fact: a year later, during Dogwood Festival time, we went to the same restaurant for dinner, and he made sure we sat in the same seats. That's where he proposed.

He was gone most of the first thirty days of our marriage; he was always in and out of the country. Anytime any of the SF dogs deployed, he'd go over there, spend time, and make sure they got acclimated and were still working well.

Kenney deployed about a week after that for only two months. Before he left, he was sure to say how much he loved me. Even the guys on his team gave him a hard time, because he talked about me all the time. Jeremy always told him he hated him for stealing his friend (meaning me). Jeremy is the one who told me Kenney was dead, even before the army notified me. He couldn't let anyone else tell me.

Kenney and I didn't have kids together; he had two sons and a daughter from his previous marriage, and I have a son and daughter from a previous marriage.

Kenney Bruce Wilson and I were only married for forty-five days. I knew him for fourteen months before that. He was Special Forces in the army for twenty-four years, and was deployed to war zones a total of nine years. He was assigned to the Operations Detachment (OPSDET), Group Support Battalion, 3d Special Forces Group (Airborne). Master Sergeant Wilson served as the kennel master for 3d Special Forces Group (Airborne). He was the operations sergeant for the kennels responsible for the health, welfare, and care of thirteen soldiers and K-9s. A book was written about one of the deployments because the battles were so serious.

When Kenney was here, we enjoyed anything that we could do together; we just loved being together. We liked car trips a lot. There are songs that really connect us. When we first met and he found out more about me, he started laughing and said, "Well, I did it; I found the perfect girl!" Then he played his ring tone for me—the song "Perfect Girl" by JB and The Moonshine Band. I had never heard it before, but the song pretty much describes me. It's never been a popular radio song, but I hear it every now and then, usually when I've had a rough day. It comes on the radio at the times I need it! The other song is "Melissa" by the Allman Brothers band.

Kenney was gone about thirty days of our short marriage. The nine deployments to war zones took its toll on him. It added up for him to about nine years of war zones out of twenty-four years of service, deployed in Africa, Iraq, and Afghanistan. He was under so much stress and carried heavy loads back from each deployment. He suffered horribly. I feel he was haunted all the time. You could see the struggle on his face. Even when he was happy, there was always something in his eyes.

I don't know how the army expects these men to do what they do and still be healthy mentally. It's horrible, honestly.

My husband died by taking his life on July 2, 2012, eleven days before his forty-fourth birthday. He shot himself, not at the house, but at a trailer he had. Two days after his passing, on July 4, my ten-year-old son took my phone and found on YouTube the video for the song "Melissa" by the Allman Brothers and said to me, "Kenney wants you to hear this song, Mom."

Kenney never played the songs in front of the kids. My son was only ten at the time and had never heard that song before. How would he even know how to find it? I know that Kenney gave my son the message. What ten-year-old knows how to search YouTube for the Allman Brothers? It was just what I needed at the time to feel even a tiny bit of peace.

I had been under an almost constant panic attack for two days at that point, obviously hiding it from my kids, but I felt as if I were constantly screaming inside. The song my son gave me made me feel like I could breathe even for a second.

My husband comes to visit me on and off; I would say probably once a week. I wake up around 2 a.m., which is about the time I believe he died. I wake up and feel him looking at me as he stands in my bedroom. He doesn't speak, and I can't see him, but I know he is there and he is always standing near his closet. I'm not sure if he is afraid to cross over, but I wish he would. I feel sad that he is still hanging on in-between.

He also visits my son, but my son can actually see him. I feel scared when he visits me, but his visits give my son much comfort. My son never really said how he looked, just that he was standing right next to him and that he was with a dog that was very nippy. Jeremy confirmed that the dog would have been Bosco, who was killed a year or so earlier. "I guess he was a 'bitey' dog."

My daughter can tell when he is in the room, too, and sometimes he scares her. Once she saw him in a hideously ugly shirt he used to wear at Easter, and once with a white jumpsuit thing.

I've also noticed on days when my heart is heavy, songs of ours will come on the radio. One day I was driving with a friend and there must have been ten songs in a row that were *our songs* with not one commercial between. Even my friend thought that was crazy.

The song "A Woman Like You" by Lee Brice comes into my radar often. Kenney often played it for me while we were getting ready in the mornings, and sang it to me. That always makes me smile and think of him.

He has visited me in places other than our house; I can feel him staring at me although I can never see him or smell him. It's always at night when I wake with a strong overwhelming feeling. The very first time I had that feeling was the third week in September; we were at the beach on vacation, about two months after he died.

Kenney loved his dogs, all the dogs he had trained and watched over. They are together forever. He loved his working dog Rocco. He'd deny it and call him a *tool* and never a *dog*, but you could tell how much they loved each other. He accidentally shot Rocco in the tail during a mission and they had to amputate it. It was like Kenney had shot one of his buddies. I don't even think Rocco noticed!

After Kenney died, they had to retire Rocco. He wouldn't work for anyone else. I believe he went to a police officer in Pennsylvania.

Chad and Stephanie

(Army Cpl. Chad D. Groepper, as told by his wife, Stephanie)

"The pieces of my heart are missing you
When you are gone."

—Avril Lavigne

I met Chad on January 20, 2006. I still remember that week clearly. January 17 was my twentieth birthday, and my mom took me birthday shopping. As we were leaving Target, my mom asked what I wanted for my birthday and, being the smart aleck I am, I responded with, "a decent man." I think my guardian angels had a birthday surprise set up for me after hearing that.

Two days later, I was picking up my best friend to hang out. As I pulled up to her house, my cell phone rang with a number I didn't know. I answered and the guy on the other end started talking to me like he knew me. I proceed to ask who was calling and was about to hang up when my friend, Danni, came running out of her house screaming that she was going to get a call on my phone.

After I figured out what was going on, I give the phone to Danni and she asked if I wanted to drive back out to Tacoma for a date. Danni had met a guy via MySpace, and he wanted to take her out on a date. The only problem was neither of them drove. She said that Shawn, her date, had a date for me too; I'd have to drive out there to pick them up.

Danni and I made the thirty-mile drive back and picked up the boys outside of the visitor center at Joint Base Lewis McChord. I remember thinking that this is the stuff scary movies are made of, picking up some random guys. I didn't even know their full names.

We went to dinner at Olive Garden that night. Chad, my date, didn't order dinner but only drank the drinks that Shawn, who was of age, bought for him. Chad didn't even speak much during dinner. That dinner was very awkward; my first-ever blind date, and he didn't speak! After dinner we all piled into my car to figure out what we were going to do next.

The first words I heard Chad speak were, "Hey, there's a hotel across the street; let's get some jack."

We all agreed. I stopped at the liquor store for Shawn to buy some alcohol, and we made our way to the Holiday Inn. After a few drinks for the both of us, Chad finally started opening up and actually talked to me. We were both raised with the same values and morals, which is hard to find anymore. I remember the exact moment I fell in love with him. He was talking about life on the farm, and I could relate to what he was saying. We sat across from each other, and I put my leg on his. He was full of energy, full of life. He loved to ride his dirt bike and be in the outdoors.

The next three nights, we all met up and went to the hotel to hang out and drink. After those first three nights, the guys had to go into the field for three days. Those were the longest three days ever. The night they were supposed to return, I remember telling Danni, "There's something different about this boy. I think I'm in love with him."

I don't think anyone understood the connection we had until they finally got to know Chad and saw what we shared. We were married just a few months after we met—on March 20, 2006. I knew my parents wouldn't understand, because they didn't know him very well yet, so I hid it from them, until they noticed my name change. But by that time, they knew Chad and knew how well we were together.

Chad and Stephanie

Chad deployed April 2007, just two weeks after finding out I was pregnant with our first child. Our daughter, Clarissa Renee, was born a month early via emergency C-section, but Chad was able to come home to meet her when she was four weeks old. After two weeks' leave, he had to return to his unit in Iraq, where he was killed by small arms fire on February 17, 2008, in Baqubah, Iraq. He was twenty-one years old.

After Chad's death I received a few messages that I know without a doubt were messages from him. The first was about six months after his death; it came in a dream. In the dream there was a telephone ringing. I picked it up and heard, "I'm all right," he said.

"I need to see you. Show me you are all right," I said.

"You're not ready to see me yet. I love you and, rest assured, I am all right."

Some experiences happen randomly and when I need to feel him the most. It will be eighty degrees outside when I will feel a cold hand on me. Sometimes it will be on my shoulder; other times it will be on my leg or back. The isolation of the coldness lets me know that I'm not just getting goose bumps from something else. It is him.

Another incident happened recently. While Chad was in Iraq, he caught a pigeon. He was part of a group that was on watch and ... well ... they were bored. In the area was a hut thingy and a pigeon was near it. Chad managed to catch the pigeon (I have it both on video and pictures). After his death, at the beginning of the month, a pigeon began perching on my house and sitting in my yard. I tried to chase it away numerous times, but it likes my house. It wasn't until I tried to catch the pigeon, and it let me get super close, that I remembered Chad's encounter with the pigeon in Iraq. It was also at that time that I learned I am terrified of birds. We haven't seen a pigeon in a few days now, but I know that was a message.

I know Chad is also with my nieces. My daughter doesn't seem to notice or point out things, but my nieces have had experiences, one of which is unexplainable. My youngest niece, Kenzie, was not born before Chad died. One day, as she was taking a shower by herself, her mom walked past the bathroom and heard her talking. She listened for a minute and heard my niece talking to Uncle Chad and using his name. My sister-in-law walked into the bathroom and saw no one, but Kenzie insists that she was talking to Uncle Chad.

As for a song, we never had a song, considering we never had a big wedding, which was something that Chad wanted to do when he returned home. That never happened. The song that comes to mind when I think about him and our relationship would be Avril Lavigne's song "When You're Gone." He made a slide show for my birthday while he was deployed, and he added that song. Chad and I both loved music, and we each had our songs for the other person. I could make a list about a hundred pages long of songs that remind me of him or bring back memories.

During the first few years after his death, I had a hard time listening to the radio because songs like Carrie Underwood's "Just a Dream" would come on and I would break down crying. I am very thankful that Chad loved music and expressed himself through music as I did. It gives us a better connection now. Songs come on the radio and bring back memories and emotions that I feel help keep us connected.

Shawn and Stephanie

(Sgt. Shawn Dostie, as told by his wife, Stephanie)

*"I can only imagine what my eyes will see
When your face is before me
I can only imagine."*

—MercyMe

I met Shawn Dostie when I was a freshman at the University of Tennessee, Knoxville campus. It was March in the spring of 1993. We met in a pretty comical way. I was on my way back to my apartment with my roommate, driving a convertible with the top down, when I stopped at a red light. A car pulled up next to us, and Shawn and two other soldiers jumped right into our car! I thought they were carjackers!

Shawn was one of those soldiers, visiting with his unit to honor a fellow veteran at a funeral in Knoxville. I didn't even go out with him until six months later. We finally began dating, mostly long distance, and had seen each other only five or six times. Impulsively, on a Friday night, we decided we would be married at the courthouse in town on Monday morning.

We did our "courting" after we were married. He was a total romantic. I like to say he came into my life as quickly as he left. I was blessed to have a husband who was not only my best friend, but also one who always made me feel loved and special. When I was working at the Education Center in Italy, Shawn would come by and take me to lunch or have lunch with me in my office. He randomly placed chocolate roses in the driver's seat of my car.

Shawn had signed up for the army in 1991 for the 2nd Battalion, 2nd Degree Infantry Division, knowing it would place him in peril. He was stationed at Fort Campbell, north of Knoxville, when we met. He was making a career of the army and advanced quickly by taking every kind of specialized training he could sign up for.

His work was in the infantry when he received orders for training in Italy and Germany. I remember taking him to the airport when he had orders for Italy. At that time, dependents were not allowed to join the soldier overseas unless he had housing arranged; this was before 9/11. I could accompany him to check-in, and we headed for the terminal to wait for him to board the plane. We sat down for a few minutes and then he said he had forgotten something in the car, and he'd be right back. His plane took off, and I cried all the way back to the car. I opened the car door and found a dozen roses on the driver's seat with a card, "I am always with you, Stephanie, and you will join me soon." There was a special necklace draped on the steering wheel.

There were romantic memories, including gondola rides in Venice, that just continued with him. "I Can Only Imagine" by MercyMe was Shawn's favorite song. The lyrics were about imagining what it would be like to stand before God in heaven.

The American Forces Network did a show when Shawn was there for special fire training. During one radio show where soldiers recorded clips for audiences back in northern Italy, Vicenza, Shawn made it a point to get on the show and leave messages for me. "I'm Staff Sgt. Shawn Dostie, stationed in Vicenza, Italy. I'd like to say, 'Oh' to my wife, Stephanie. I love you and miss you and I'll be home soon!"

He was silly and romantic. I was lucky to have a husband who was my best friend and made me feel loved and special. Shawn was very sarcastic. He had a kind of humorous sarcasm. He liked to embarrass me. I could be standing looking out our front door as I drank my morning tea, and he would walk up behind me and "pants" me. Meaning he would pull my yoga pants down, knowing I had tea in my hands and was unable to get them up fast. He'd do other things, like walk up behind me and make a loud noise to scare me, or hide underneath the bed and grab my leg when I walked by.

I was always self-conscious, so I never let him see me naked. He would hide under the bed or, if I was in the shower, he'd sneak in and hold a mirror over the top of the shower trying to catch a peek. We'd also catch each other in the shower and pour ice water over the top on each other. He liked to dance in his underwear with his army socks pulled all the way up to his knees. (That was always the kids' favorite.)

He often surprised me when I was working at the Educational Center in Italy by bringing lunch or taking me out to lunch! He randomly put chocolate roses in the driver's seat of my car. Throughout our marriage he brought home flowers! I could not predict what night he would bring them, always on a different day. He seemed intuitively to know when I needed the flowers most.

Shawn always called before leaving work every day to ask me if I needed him to bring anything home. We were blessed with two beautiful children, Cameron and Bayleigh, and two cats that Shawn adored. This was a man who cried when the kids were born. When the kids were under the age of three, days could get very crazy. On tough days, Shawn knew how I felt by the tone of my voice, and he'd show up at the door with ice cream. Without changing his uniform, he'd tell the kids to "Give mommy a hug and kiss and tell her you love her," and for me to go relax for a while. Then he'd take them straight out the door to the park behind our living quarters so I could relax. He always knew when I needed support.

2005/12/24

Prior to Shawn deploying, he and I had both had dreams about his life being lost during the deployment. I had a similar dream about a year before it happened. He had a dream about four months before his death, which he would not share with me. We both had this foreboding. When I had my dream, I told Shawn we needed to talk about his wishes in case he didn't return. We had that talk. We had just celebrated our tenth anniversary.

Shawn was headed to a mission in Baghdad in September 2005. On December 30, I awoke suddenly at 3:33 a.m. EST (12:33 Iraq time) from a dead sleep. I immediately reached for my laptop. We connected often. I had not heard from Shawn for two days, and I had a bad feeling when I awoke so suddenly that morning. The TV was set on CNN and I kept refreshing my e-mail every twenty minutes for any news, hoping that he had returned from a convoy and would make it to the computers before dinner.

At 5:30 a.m. the ticker on CNN read "Breaking News: A U.S. soldier has been killed. The soldier was patrolling a main supply route near Baghdad when he was fatally wounded by a roadside bomb." Something in my heart told me this was Shawn. I just knew it. At that moment I knew my Shawn was gone. It was a strong knowingness. My intuition told me it was true.

I spent the rest of the morning in panic. When my children, ages five and eight, woke up that morning, I told them, "No one is to go downstairs or answer the front door." I knew the military would be at my door that day to notify me, and I didn't want my children to answer it. At 2:30 p.m., my children ran down the stairs of our on-post housing, yelling, "Mommy, someone is here." From their bedrooms they had heard the car doors slam. By the time I had made it to the top of the stairs, my children had opened our front door and started to scream.

We never concealed anything from our children and when they asked before the deployment what would happen if Daddy was hurt, we told them the truth. "Soldiers would come to the door and tell Mommy." I later found out the time of Shawn's death was 12:33 p.m. (Iraq time), the exact time, 3:33 a.m. (US time) when I woke from my sleep and was panicking. It was eight days before his thirty-third birthday.

I retreated to my room while the chaplain and notifying officer were downstairs. I wanted to sit on our bed and smell his pillow. I remember holding it and screaming, "Shawn, Shawn!" Here is the amazing part: after a few minutes, I felt a squeezing of my left hand that lasted about ten seconds. It was a firm but comforting squeeze. It felt real. It was like Shawn was grabbing my hand and saying, "It's okay, I'm here." And then all of a sudden, it was gone. I know it was him.

There was another message from Shawn. It was a couple of days after he was killed, when my best friend called me and said she had a dream about Shawn. My friend said, "I walked into what I thought was a church. It was empty except for one soldier sitting in a pew. As I walked down the center aisle and was even with the row where the soldier sat, Shawn stood up and looked at me. He was wearing his military uniform, except the color of the uniform was red. It was Shawn. He looked at me and said, 'Take care of Steph.'" She couldn't understand why his uniform was red in the dream, but found out weeks later that Shawn's body had been burning inside his upside-down vehicle for hours.

I loved the scent of Shawn's cologne. When I was attending the University of Tennessee and he was in Kentucky, after visiting each other, I sprayed his cologne on my pillow so I could take a piece of Shawn home with me after we had been together. Months following his death, I could walk through our house near the base and smell his cologne in certain areas of the house. It only lasted for three to five seconds, but I would smell him. He wore a distinctive cologne called Drakker that had a woody, aromatic, fresh spicy, earthy, balsamic, citrus fragrance. I cannot mistake it for anything else.

The smell would also appear in certain areas of the house in Tennessee after he died. When I walked past the curio cabinet with all his memorabilia in it, I could smell the distinct cologne outside the cabinet, as if he were there. It would last about three to five seconds. He wore two colognes; the second one is called Cool Water. It is described as "The mood of the sea, the spirit of the wind; for the man who lives each day to its fullest." Clean and refreshing, it reflects a man's active lifestyle with a blend of lavender, menthe, sandalwood, iris, and musk. It is distinct. He wore those two colognes, both distinctive and so affirming to me. It was him! I have no doubt!

My in-laws had come for the two weeks after Shawn's death and slept in our living room where our grandfather clock was hanging. Engraved on the pendulum was our last name and wedding date. When they moved us into our house six months earlier, the movers didn't know how to install the weights, so the pendulum hadn't been working since then. However, every night, the clock chimed, waking up my father-in-law. He questioned me about the clock not working, yet it chimed! I had no answers for him. It had not made a noise in the previous six months, but since Shawn was gone, it had begun chiming at night. I knew this was another sign from Shawn.

We had purchased Persian cats in Italy in 1996, Paris and Vicenza. Paris was Shawn's cat. He told me before he left that if anything seemed wrong with Paris, to make sure I had the vet check her out. She was his baby, and he wanted to make sure she was still there when he returned from Iraq. About two months after Shawn's death, I was petting her and felt a lump on her neck. I made an appointment and found out she had cancer. I had told the vet to do anything to keep her alive, so we scheduled surgery. They removed the cancer, but six months later she became sick again. I took her back to the vet and was told the cancer had spread, and she was suffering. She never left the clinic that day, and I had Paris cremated.

A couple of months later, my in-laws flew to Washington, DC, and met me at Arlington. Shawn's headstone had finally arrived and I was going to take a small shovel and bury Paris's ashes by Shawn's stone. However, there were funerals daily; the ground was too hard, and there were so many people in Section 60 that it was impossible to bury her. My in-laws were flying home the next day, so we opted to pull the grass away from the back of Shawn's stone and pour her ashes there. My father-in-law then took some water and poured it over the ashes so they wouldn't fly away. My friends were flying into DC the following day and we all headed back to Arlington with fresh flowers for his grave.

While cutting the flowers in front of his stone, my friend asked, "Steph, what was left of Paris when you brought her out here?"

"Just ashes and there were a few pieces of bone. Why do you ask?"

"You have to see this!" I walked to the back of the stone and there was grayish-blue cat hair everywhere. I couldn't believe what I was seeing. I took pictures and sent them to my mother- and father-in-law and they were just as speechless. Over the years, we have considered that to be a sign from Shawn; Paris was with him now.

There have been things that my children have seen. On the first day of school after their dad was killed, they were standing on the sidewalk in front of the house. I had forgotten something and ran back into the house. When I walked back outside, they were both standing almost frozen, white as ghosts, with this blank look on their faces. I paused for a sec, and then asked, "What's wrong?"

"Daddy was standing inside the door and waving at us. He is wearing his physical training uniform, basically black shorts and gray shirt with the army logo on it, and a yellow reflector belt. We saw him, Mommy, it was Daddy!"

Another time, my five-year-old daughter ran downstairs crying after playing in her room. She said, "Daddy is in my closet and his nose is bleeding." I just hugged her.

Even now, eight years later, I have "bad days." I think about the what-ifs, and the what it would be like if life had not changed. I wonder if his hair would be gray or if he would have as many wrinkles around the corners of his eyes as I do. I think about where we would be geographically and if he would have chosen to retire from the army at twenty years or chose to stay in another four to six years. I know I would be different if he were still here.

I don't think I would appreciate every day given to the kids and me, like I do now, had I not experienced losing the closest thing to my heart in 2005. I stop and listen to birds sing and don't hurry as quickly to get out of the rain. I try to take in everyone and everything around me and enjoy them for who they are or what it is. I'm not the same person I was when he was alive; a part of me died with him. I will never be *her* again, that passive, quiet woman who said yes to everything so she could please people. I learned to be the woman who stands up for herself, speaks up when I don't agree, and walks away from toxic people. I didn't have him there to do that for me anymore, so I learned to do it to protect myself and my children. It made me think back to 1995, newly married and young, with no responsibility or care in the world except being together every second of the day.

I sense him around me all the time. When I ask him for strength, he sends it to me. Just this morning, while taking my kids to school, I was sitting at a red light. A couple pulled up in the lane next to us. They were young. He was a soldier, and it looked like he was heading into work. She was possibly dropping him off and keeping the car, like most of us have had to do starting off, car sharing with neighbors. We could come and go as we pleased, not yet needing thirty extra minutes to get kids in and out of car seats or running back into the house to get the diaper bag we had forgotten.

"Together Again" by Janet Jackson began to play on the radio. It was released in 1997, the same year our first child was born. Of course, it made me cry, but I also knew he was sending me a "wink " to let me know he was seeing/hearing every thought running through my mind. It brought me comfort just like every other time he sends me a sign.

Together Again

"Everywhere I go ...
I know you are there,
Smilin' back at me."

—Janet Jackson

Vito and His Daughter, Ariel

(L.Cpl. Vita Lapinta, talking about his daughter Ariel)

"I know I'll think of you every step of the way."

—Whitney Houston

I was stationed in Columbia, working with Reagan's Just Say No mission. I was a marine, 3rd lance corporal, Special Forces, Reconnaissance, four years in the service. After we would nix one drug factory and know there were others close by, we were told to do nothing. Weird and confusing. I couldn't understand how we had to walk away when we knew of drug cartels so close to us.

My best pal died right next to me, killed by a sniper. I held him in my arms and I was very choked up. When gunfire exploded, I had to leave him there. It could have been me.

PTSD rips at me because of these ruthless experiences. It is hard not to be upset just remembering those times.

I am lucky to be the proud dad of three children, two daughters and a son.

While you may think I had experiences from those who died during war conflicts, it was on my return to the States when I had the strangest experience.

I had been estranged from my daughter Ariel for several years. I tried to connect with her, but to no avail; I could not locate her. I tried desperately to reach her, but nothing worked.

It was on the November Election Day for Obama that I was sitting at the computer in my study when I heard a female voice. My son was in the other room. "Dad, it's Ariel's voice, clear and vibrant," he called out.

I looked around, opened closets and looked under beds, and saw nothing. Still, I knew it was Ariel's voice. I was baffled; it seemed she was there, somewhere close in the room. I found out about a month later that Ariel had died on that Election Day of a very rare cancer called Ewing's cancer. The disease attacks the bones and tissues and is often found in teenagers and young adults. It was the same day she was calling for me. I felt devastated.

About a month later, I was working in my room and my son, Vito Junior, was working in another room, separated by a stairwell between the two rooms. We both vividly heard a voice. I jumped up from my computer and my son also jumped up, and we both headed to the top of the stairwell.

"Dad, where are you?" came Ariel's voice, clear as a whistle; I knew it.

My son shouted out from his room, "Dad, did you hear that?"

"Yes, I heard her."

We both ran to the stairwell, and I looked at my son, and my son said in disbelief, "Dad, that was Ariel's voice!"

"Yes, it was her voice."

I still become choked up telling about the experience. "I have no doubt it was my daughter."

I will always carry my daughter in my heart. She has never left me and I have never left her. I know she came through to say goodbye.

Golden Threads

In our nights and in our days they are with us.
They walk leading our path to familiar places.
Words come and go.
Faces appear and disappear,
Smiling and silent,
Speaking in thoughts,
They turn and go.
Golden threads connect us forever.

—Maureen McGill

David and August

(Lt. Col. David E. Cabrera, as told by his wife, August)

"We'll enter in as the wedding bells ring;
Your bride will come together and we'll sing ..."
—Paul Wickman

I met David Cabrera October 19, 2001, at a costume party. I knew within fifteen minutes of meeting David that I would marry him, even though everyone was in costume. Everyone wore hats and masks at this party; it wasn't until the end of the evening when the hats came off that I realized David had the army haircut, along with every other fellow at the party.

He had a stupid haircut that shouted, "You're in the army!"

We flirted with each other. I found out he was divorced and was a devoted father of two children. He had a long list of pedigrees, undergraduate degree in psychology, Texas A&M, and eventually a PhD in social work. He was a romantic. The romance just kept on going!

One year after the day we met, we spontaneously decided to get married at the Ritz Carleton Hotel on a Saturday night, where one can fall asleep in the towels. On a Friday night, we looked for a minister online. The one we found said, "I have four weddings that day, and the last one is at the Ritz tomorrow, so meet me at the bar afterwards, and we will go upstairs to a room which might be available from the previous wedding!"

We met the minister at the bar. I wore my hiking boots and a long skirt, and David wore a blue turtleneck. It was very casual.

A couple of close friends were with us as witnesses when we tied the knot, as another wedding celebrated in loud jubilation in the adjacent room. We ended up going out to dinner and then to the movie, *My Big Fat Greek Wedding*. There was a lot of laughter!

David, a true romantic, loved weddings, and married me again on a summer day. He wanted his two children with us, ages four and five. The setting was a warm July day in 2003 when we exchanged vows next to a creek. He loved reliving the ceremony with me.

We had some conflict on liking the same kind of music, but we had a song we both loved and connected with, called "You're Beautiful" sung by Paul Wickman.

Our lives unfolded. David was a full-time active soldier and juggled deployments and different duty stations. Our son Max was born in 2004 then I went back to the university for my master's in public administration. We managed careers and school in preparation for the birth of Roanin, who was born in 2006. That same year David deployed to Iraq.

Six weeks prior to David's deployment he blindfolded me and proposed again with a beautiful ring. We renewed our vows at a friend's private dock.

In July 2007, David was stationed in Germany, and we moved our family overseas. It did not stop David from arranging yet another wedding ceremony.

"Happy surprise birthday, August!" It was my thirty-fifth birthday.

"Pack your bag, we are getting married in Heidelberg Castle, and we are doing a double ceremony with our best friends!"

My girlfriend and I had five days to plan a wedding! Our grooms wore their dress-blue uniforms. My friend and I looked through our military ball gowns and found black dresses. I wore a short black cocktail dress, and she wore a long black gown. We got married at the castle, with the kids present! We dined at a restaurant on the Haupt Strasse.

David was promoted to lieutenant colonel on September 1, 2011, in a small ceremony at Uniformed Services Health Sciences University, surrounded by his family, friends, and close colleagues. He left for deployment to Afghanistan on September 23, and left the States on October 1. He was with his therapy dog, Lucy, whom he brought with him to help others.

About a month after he left, on Saturday morning, October 29, 2011, I woke up at 2 a.m. and sat up in bed. Something told me I needed to pray for David. At 4:11 a.m., our five-year-old son, who slept in the bedroom, woke up screaming.

"I had a dream there was a terrible explosion and everyone died in the fire, Mommy," he told me.

It took a long time to calm him down. I e-mailed David and received no replies, several e-mails more and still no replies! Later that day, I was reading the *Huffington Post News*, and saw the headline, "NATO Convoy Hit Outside of Kabul, 17 killed." I knew it was David.

He was heading to another base on October 29 when a van packed with explosives and driven by a suicide bomber swerved into the Rhino. The explosion killed a Canadian soldier, one civilian member of the Department of Defense, seven contractors, and four US soldiers, including my husband. The blast also killed an Afghan police officer and four Afghan civilians, including three children, and Lucy, David's therapy dog.

We had an agreement that if anything horrible happened, a colleague of David's would be notified in DC. I just waited for the dreaded car to appear in the driveway twenty-four hours later. It arrived. I screamed, "No!" That was the beginning of the end for me.

I went through four memorial services, with no experience of sensing David. Nothing, until six months after he died, I had this dream:

I dreamt I was in a spa, like Europe. David had acne scars on his face in real life; when he walked in and I saw him in my dream, his face was clear, not a blemish, but pure, soft, and smooth. He was wearing an all-white linen shirt and white pants. His face looked so pure.

"It's okay," he said.

"You have to go back!" I asked.

"It is okay," he said. "We have a few minutes." And then he kissed me, so beautiful and so real. I could feel his lips touch mine; I know it was him.

After he died in 2011, I would get to these places where I felt so upset, I would shout out loud, "Why did you do this to me? I need to know you are still there. Please give me a sign, anything." Within minutes the song "You're Beautiful" came on the radio, over and over, our song!

It was a year later that I went to church on the condition in my mind I would not hear that song played. It was spring 2012. Right before I went to church, I said to David, "Show up, dammit, show up."

A few months later, I attended a compelling worship service about letting go of anger, and I saw that the song "You're Beautiful" was on the docket. It was not even a song that corresponded to the sermon. I asked the music director, "Why did you choose that song?"

"I don't know, it just came to me," she responded.

I found e-mails after David died; he had planned yet another wedding in Las Vegas. He wrote, "Will you marry me when I get home?" But David never returned home for the final wedding. Still, the song continues to come to me at odd times.

"I see your power in the moonlit night ...
It's all proclaiming who You are."

—Phil Wickham

Steven and Elizabeth

(MSgt. Steven A. Monnin, as told by his wife, Elizabeth)

"Faithfully
I'm still yours,
Ever yours."

—Journey

My husband's name is MSgt. Steven A. Monnin, US Air Force. "Faithfully" by Journey was one of our songs when we dated back in the '80s.

MSgt. Steven A. Monnin, US Air Force, Persian Gulf War, 92nd Civil Engineer Squadron, married me, Elizabeth Hill. Both of us were the same age, born fourteen hours apart, that same day, same year. We were both eighteen when we met, the summer after high school graduation. We worked at Burger King. He asked me out, but I had to take a rain check.

When we started dating, July 14, 1987, it was love at first sight. I told my grandpa I was going to marry Steven, and that there was something weird about his birthday. It wasn't until our second date that we found out that our birthdays were exactly the same.

When Steven left for basic training on September 17, 1987, he asked me to marry him when he returned. We were married the next year, on September 10, 1988.

We had three sons, Anthony, Andrew, and Nicholas, and a daughter Christiana. Steven was active as a Boy Scout leader, volunteered as a mentor with the Big Brother/Big Sister program, and participated in Habitat for Humanity. He also coached several Little League teams throughout the years.

He served in the air force, working as an electrician and then in an administration job. Steven was around a lot when the kids were young, but was deployed for long periods of time when our oldest son was in junior high.

Steven faced anger issues and just plain rage, with no patience. I had to hold a full-time job, pay all the bills, care for the house and our four children while he was gone. He had a history of family mental illness, but the deployments took an additional toll. I don't think it helped that he took body-building aids when he was deployed, something I think contributed to his emotional instability. He was in the service for seventeen years.

There was no base counseling when he returned from his deployment. His anger escalated to bouts of yelling and emotionally abusing us. He received a felony ticket for road rage. He had just started anger management and couple's therapy when he took his life, after one year of returning from a deployment.

That was eleven years ago. Soon after he died, Steven connected with me; it was a strong feeling. I saw my husband in a dream; he was dying and I could do nothing to stop it. In another dream, he knocked at the front door and was standing there. He looked sad, around thirty-five years old, and very much alive again.

In the dream, it was a few years later, and we were all angry at him for making us believe he was dead. I knew he was nearby. I would ask for a sign or something, and he sent me pennies to find in the weirdest places. His pennies are always facing down; my grandpa sends them face up. I know it is Steven when I find the pennies.

He lets me know how he missed me.

I had a dream where I went back to the place where he died; the door opened and with a whoosh of air right at me, he appeared. I saw him, vibrant and strong.

"I miss you," he said.

I knew it was him in the dream, I could just feel it. The owner of the house could not see him, only me.

It has been a long journey. Two years after Steven's death, I had been gone from the house one evening for only two hours, and when I returned, my son, Andy, had killed himself. I found him in my closet. It was the worst night of my life.

Even though life can be filled with darkness, there is good in all life. A man who lived nearby became an angel for us. He helped me with the house and so many things. We became friends about a year after Steven's death in 2006 and we started dating. Eventually, in 2010, we got married. I believe Steven brought Brian to our lives.

One thing that happened recently was receiving another message from Steven. I was in a serious car accident. I had just remarried at the time of the accident, and it had been nine years since Steven died. I had major surgery and when I woke up, I was calling, "Steven!"

I believe he came to me while I was in surgery. It was something I asked out loud, "Am I okay now, Steven?"

"You are okay," he said.

I think … I know he helped save me from dying at that time. I woke up feeling very hopeful and strong! I knew Steven's message was a healing message for me.

I attended a Snowball Express Fair before Christmas. The event was an annual trip for gold star children in Dallas, Texas. There was an older lady attending a quilt booth. It was a memory quilt, and I was looking for my husband's name when she told me, "The quilt is for heroes and Steven doesn't qualify because he died by suicide stateside."

I cried almost instantly! I was shocked that she said that to my face! This is what widows face—the judgment, the criticism, and the journey of veterans in this work.

Another song that was ours is "I Guess That's Why They Call It the Blues," by Elton John. The words "don't wish it away … things can only get better" ring true to me.

Kevin and Theresa

(Army Master Sgt. Kevin Morehead, as told by his wife, Theresa)

"If tomorrow never comes
Will she know how much I loved her?"

—Garth Brooks

I met Kevin Morehead at a country bar, on a Thursday night. I went with my girlfriend to see this band, Shenandoah. I saw him walk in the door and just stand still there; he had on jeans, roper boots, and a blue-and-white-striped shirt. I wore jeans and a shirt. As soon as I saw him, I told my girlfriend, "I am going to marry that man!" I felt something in my heart that I never felt before ... with anyone!

"Go talk to him."

"I'm afraid. I'm going through a divorce and haven't dated anyone in over fifteen years. I am too nervous."

Well, I got the nerve up and went up to him. "May I buy you a Coca-Cola?" As soon as those words left my lips, I thought I totally blew it!

"A Coca-Cola? What the *what?* Sure! My name is Kevin!"

So I bought the coke, took it to him, and walked away, knowing I totally blew it.

Later that night he came over to me, bought me a beer, and handed it to me. "Can I sit down?" he asked.

He sat. We talked for a while.

"I have two beautiful daughters," I told him.

"Well, that is good, because I do not want to have any kids."

"I can't have any more kids because I had my tubes tied."

"That's fine with me," Kevin shared.

"You know what, Kevin, it's getting late and I have to get up for work tomorrow morning, so I have to leave here right away. I'm going to ask my girlfriend if she's ready to leave."

"I am not leaving now," my girlfriend said. "Go ahead."

"Can I take you to your car?" Kevin offered.

"How do I know you're not a mass murderer?"

He laughed. "I'm not going to kill you! Ha-ha-ha!"

He walked me to my car and I would not give him my number, but he gave me his.

It took me two weeks to call him. When I did, he invited me to his house for dinner. He cooked for me! From that night on, we were never apart until he was selected to be in Special Forces. I was sad because he was moving. He said he'd figure out a way for us to see each other and he did!

We met once a month in either Gatlinburg or Knoxville and would spend the weekend together. One morning he woke up and said, "Let's go get married!"

"Can we go shopping instead?" I just had gone through a divorce and was not ready for marriage again, but something inside of me could not say no.

I was madly in love with Kevin. I would have done anything for him. He was twenty-four and I was thirty-three. On April 1, 1995, we became husband and wife, married by a justice of the peace in a little rundown motel in the lobby. They were doing repairs and another couple was waiting to get married. There were no flowers or fluff. He wore jeans and a polo shirt, and I wore jeans, a white-striped shirt, and mountain boots. It wasn't much, but we were married and we were very happy. Three years later, he surprised me with a wedding in a beautiful chapel nestled in the woods on the edge of a mountain. He planned it all by himself. On the way out of town, we stopped at the mall and he bought me a wedding dress, which I still have, and he bought a suit. It was beautiful and we renewed our vows on April 23, 1998, and stayed at a lovely B&B that night.

Kevin was a romantic. Once he sent roses to me at my work, with a card inviting me to dinner that evening. I still have the card. He enjoyed playing his favorite song, "If Tomorrow Never Comes," on his guitar.

After the wedding Kevin was stationed in Clarkesville, Tennessee, a medic with the 5th Group Special Forces, Green Beret. He stayed with his aunt and uncle, and eventually got a studio apartment. He wanted me to move there after we were married; I was still in Fayetteville and finally decided to quit my job and the rest is history.

We purchased the smallest country house outside of Clarkesville, with low ceilings, small rooms, and a porch swing. Kevin started reconsidering the possibility of having a child, and we discussed the road to a reversal operation since my tubes were tied. He took the lead in making medical appointments, and I eventually became pregnant. The road to having our little girl was not easy. On a quiet snowy winter day, after only five months of pregnancy, our daughter Taylor became an angel in heaven. I ended up having physical complications ending in a near-death experience a few days after she was born. In the experience, I felt this moment of peace with God. All fear was gone. My whole body radiated in peacefulness. Kevin went out and bought our little angel a beautiful dress for her cremation. She is an angel now, and sleeps at the edge of my bed, where she remains.

After that time we became even closer despite his deployments overseas, Pakistan, Kuwait, Djibouti, and then finally Kevin's last assignment to Iraq.

On the day he was leaving for the plane, we were rushing around the house packing for him.

"I can't find my Bible," he said. "I am not leaving without one. I have to have it!"

We ran out of time and, on the way to the post, we stopped at Walmart and bought one for him to take on the trip.

I had heard from Kevin on 9/10/03 in an e-mail that he would be gone for twenty-two days. It was the morning of 9/11/03 that I was feeling uncomfortable. I had received an anniversary card in the mail that I had sent to Kevin in March for our eighth wedding anniversary. I e-mailed Kevin on 9/11/03 to tell him the card was returned to me. He did not respond. A friend on the computer chat told me not to worry, as servers are often down and messages are delayed.

Early the morning of 9/12/03, I was reading the newspaper online. "Two soldiers were killed in AR Ramadi." My heart began to sink. I went out to the garage and pleaded with God in prayer.

"Please, don't let it be him. Please, God, don't let it be him." I was crying nonstop. I took deep breaths and prepared to go to work. About two hours later, I heard the tap at the door. I guessed it was the bus drivers ready for work. Instead, through the window I saw four uniformed soldiers about to bring the sad news. My world stopped at that moment.

Kevin was in AR Ramadi and was scaling a wall when he tried to cross to the other side. Al Queda tossed an improvised explosive device between his feet. The device exploded as he tried to get away. The bullet hit the seam of his bulletproof vest and pierced his heart. He was thirty-three years old. It happened on 9/11/03, the same day our anniversary card was returned. Maybe it was a message from him that the card was returned that same day. I knew he was with Taylor in heaven, the place of unconditional love, when I heard Jason Crabb, the country singer who sang "I Sure Miss You" at his funeral. The words, "Life will never be the same with you not here," provided God's grace to keep me strong.

I have never remembered my dreams much, but I swear I had two visitation dreams since Kevin's passing. The first dream was about a month after he died.

Kevin was sitting in a green, putrid hospital room. He was in the hospital bed with a gown and no covers. I was begging him to wake up. "Please wake up, please wake up." I kept up the pleading.

At that moment he sat up, his legs dangling over the bedside.

"You're wrong, Kevin is not dead; he is coming home."

At that moment he opened his eyes and he stared at me, his pupils appearing in the shape of crosses. I said, "I knew you would come back, I knew you would come back. "

He looked straight ahead at me, like a robot, and these words came from him: "I love you, I love you." I heard his voice whisper in my ear. I heard him clearly. His voice was very real. He put his feet back up on the bed and closed his eyes. Then I started crying, "Don't leave me, don't leave me."

About eleven years later, in 2014, I received a request to speak to a medic who had been with Kevin in those last moments. It had taken him many years to find me, but he was determined to speak with me. He wanted to share with me the final moments of Kevin's life, and he wanted to reassure me he did everything he could to help him survive. Kevin bled to death.

The medic described the room where Kevin lay in those final moments with him. "It was putrid yellow green," the medic said.

I could not believe that was the same room I had dreamed about right after news of his death, and the same way I described it. I had hoped there was a message from Kevin on his dying moments, but the message I received so many years later confirmed I was with him in that hospital room when he died.

I remember another dream I had a few weeks after Kevin died. I was sitting beside his casket and crying, when Kevin reached out from the casket and pulled me in to him. I could feel him hug me. It was so real, I could feel his arms wrap around me. It was so real, so real. I knew it was him.

As my life unfolded, it was a hard journey to reconnect in the dating world. It was three years later that I started dating a man I had met on the Internet after about eleven months. Richard seemed upright to me. He was a successful musician and artist, and we enjoyed each other's company. He lived in Florida, and I lived in Tennessee. He seemed kind as he told me how he sent money to a family in need at his church on a regular basis. Richard would commute to Tennessee, where we married in December 2006. We moved to South Carolina to be closer to my daughters and grandsons. He said he didn't mind moving to support my family.

We moved again about a year and a half later when I began to have suspicions about his fidelity in the marriage. I had a feeling something was wrong. It was a clear directive from above to check his phone calls and e-mails. Then I found an e-mail which stated: "You can go on with your life, but I am still your wife!"

I was speechless and did not mention this to Richard. Instead, I investigated further and found a phone number, which had repeated several calls over several months since my marriage to Richard. I traced the calls to another town with that particular repeated phone number. I decided not to confront Richard, but called the number of his so-called mistress.

"I wanted to let you know that Richard is a married man," I said.

"No, he is not, he is married to me. He left me in 2006, but he never divorced me. He sends me rent money."

When I confronted Richard, he kept denying he was married. I confirmed with court records he never got a divorce and was basically a polygamist. At that point, I was fearful and got a restraining order against this man. I was hoping the order would not be delivered when I was at the house. The police arrived only to find me in the living room and Richard at the back of the house. I was nervous. The policeman told me, "Stay in the living room and talk to me."

The policeman was kind and wanted to know about my life.

I told him, "My late husband was KIA three years ago; he is in heaven now. His name is Kevin Morehead. I married Richard, only to find out he is married to a woman in another state!"

The police officer responded, "Was that Kevin Neil Morehead?"

"Yes, that was his name."

Then the policeman kneeled down at my feet and said to me, "I had three of these memorial bracelets and gave two of them away. I have been wearing this one for three years and never took it off; it was special to me for some reason, but I didn't know why."

He pulled up his sleeve and handed me the bracelet with Kevin's name on it.

The police officer, whose name is Bear, came back a few weeks later to check on me. He said, "I am so moved by wearing Kevin's bracelet and not sure why his bracelet was the one I kept on. I wanted you to know that the night we saw you, I was driving with another officer. I told him the story and we pulled the squad car over, and we both cried. We know Kevin is with you, protecting you."

I have no doubt Kevin saved me from this criminal. He was so with me that night.

For Kevin

He walks with Baby Angel now ...

Her white dress wrapped in his arms ...

I see you in my dreams, baby ...

Always caring, always helping, always present ...

That never changes, never fades, never dies ...

Your love is here, on the porch, in the swing,

at the foot of the bed ...

At the breakfast coffee, at the Cracker Barrel table ...

In the hearts that never forget you ...

Always and Forever ...

It won't be long now, baby, we will get on with our lives ...

From this day forward ...

—Maureen McGill

A Message from Paul

(From Lt. Airman Andrew Dee, RAF)

The Leader of the Pack

*"I can't hide the tears, but I don't care,
I'll never forget him, the leader of the pack."*

—Shangri-Las

[NOTE: Andrew Dee is a former British Royal Air Force soldier. He shares his gift of mediumship to an audience. Mediumship is a formal portal of communication to the other side. —MM]

I am still intrigued by the human quest for knowledge and proof of life after physical death. We are constantly trying to make sense of our physical lives, and often turn to spirit for help. The world of spirit can help, in lots of ways. Being a spirit medium does not make life any easier for me. I still face daily challenges. It is my faith that keeps me strong. This is my purpose in this life.

It is my aim, my desire to help those who have lost direction find their way once more, with guides and loved ones by your side to help your loved ones offer you the guidance you need to find your way. It is not fortune telling; it is not about shock value; it is about using clairvoyant vision and psychic or spiritual intervention to help my clients.

I was presenting in England when I received a message for a woman in the audience. A fellow stepped into my reading from spirit during one of my sessions, with a message for her. He had a motorbike accident seventeen years earlier; it was clear he was a part of the British army, of the Royal Signals Motorbike Display Team, known as the White Helmets. He was actually a very keen motorbike rider, and I was made aware he had died on his motorbike, on an open road with a tree next to the road. I was not sure if the tree was connected to the story. He introduced himself as Paul. This later was confirmed as truth by Paul's sister.

I know he was going into a bang on the motorbike; he talked to me directly. "If I had only ridden differently; there was something on the road. There is something slippery on the road, and I cannot tell if it is oil or grease. There is a black patch of something. I thought it might be oil, but I felt I needed to separate myself from assuming it was oil or grease. It wasn't."

"Yes, you are correct," Paul's sister confirmed. "Paul would not have died on his motorbike that day, when they were racing bikes. He and three other friends had gone out on their bikes. He and his friend usually rode position two and four. That morning they decided to swap positions. And if Paul had not swapped positions … maybe it would be for his friend's benefit they made that decision."

I was very quickly taken to his funeral. I was shown how this funeral parade was planned with military precision. "There was a police escort with the funeral. Is that correct?"

"Yes," Paul's sister confirmed.

At this point I wasn't sure this was Paul in the army, but he was talking about a police escort with a ride past.

His sister confirmed. "The motorbikes that they used in display are not legal on the road. The army came on these special display bikes and had police outriders because bikes were not road legal."

I could see hundreds of people at this funeral; no one paid for a drink. It was like people were paying for the drinks in glasses, like putting money in the glasses to pay for the drinks. It was like a free-for-all; army was putting money into a pot. Vroom, vroom, they are revving the engines!

Andrew didn't know why he was showing him this revving up of engines, and then Andrew heard, "This is a salute to you, Sis."

She started crying.

Revving up the engines was what they used to do at the end of a display to salute the commanding officer or any dignitary that was watching the display. All the bikes would line up and rev their engines.

Paul just wanted to bring his love through with this message for his sister. It was the first time he had ever come to her in sixteen years since his passing! She was so happy to have this message.

A Message from Grandpa

(From Lt. Airman Andrew Dee, RAF)

"I drove all night
Crept in your room
Woke you from your sleep."

—Celine Dion

During my stay in the Royal Air Force six years ago, I was stationed in Iraq for four months. For some reason, I listened to the song "I Drove All Night" by Celine Dion over and over during the time I was there. The words stayed with me. "I drove all night to get to you... I crept in your room, woke you from sleep." You know spirit is not very far away from us.

It was a hard, hot, dusty day, and I was missing my family and friends when I was walking in the desert sand with boots on. I literally stumbled upon something under my feet. I found a very small key ring, which was a Dutch clog in the sand. I was absolutely taken back. You see, I was three thousand miles from my home in England, and I was one hundred meters from the room I was sleeping in, when I felt my grandfather's presence instantly. I could smell him.

Both of my grandfathers were Dutch, and for me to find a clog in the sand that far away from home was fairly extraordinary. My father owned a restaurant called Clogs Men. My mom, who at seventy still owns the pub, still pulls pints! We have a collection of clogs, all from our family in Holland, which are mounted all the way up the wall of the pub. There is no doubt this was a message from my grandfather. What were the chances for me to find a clog in the middle of the desert?

He was with me; I have no doubt!

Joseph and Angie

(Spc. Joseph M. Blickenstaff, as told by his wife, Angie)

"I know someday you'll have a beautiful life,
I know you'll be a sun in somebody else's sky,
But, why, why, why can't you be mine?"

—Pearl Jam

I was introduced to Joe, US Army Specialist Joseph M. Blickenstaff, by a mutual friend. We were young. Joe had joined the army barely out of high school and was based at Fort Lewis, Washington, when I met him. He was struggling in high school, and the army helped him focus and find discipline in his life.

Joe was away for the weekend when he and his buddy stopped over at my friend's apartment in Corvallis, Oregon, and the rest is history. We didn't hit it off until we heard this band on the radio—Collective Soul—and we both loved their music! The band music took the best of what grunge could offer and brought the sound up one notch!

Joe was incredibly passionate about music and subsequently introduced me to many bands that I love. He even kept his CD player in his camelback during the missions.

[69]

We couldn't seem to stop talking to each other after the first meeting. We drove to the Oregon coast for our first date and walked the beach holding hands. After that we were inseparable. I'd never met any guy I could talk to so easily. We would stay up from night until late morning hours just talking! We had dated less than a year when he decided to join the US Army.

Joe had just graduated army basic training and infantry training and came home for a few days to Albany, Oregon, when the September 11 attacks occurred. We drove around Albany, looking for a place to donate blood. He reported to Fort Lewis a week later.

We decided to get married on October 6, 2001, and I moved up to Washington State in December. We moved into an apartment in Steilacoom. There was definitely a deep, deep connection between us. Our wedding day was amazing. We had a very small, private wedding in a friend's beautiful yard near a lake, not far from the base. Joe wore his army dress uniform and looked very handsome. I truly felt like that day was the most special day of my entire life. It felt like a fairytale.

I had so much innocence with Joe. We were both young. Most of all, I remember his hugs. Something about being held in his embrace made everything else melt away, even our own troubles. He was an old soul. Ten years later, I still feel our relationship and the time we spent together, both good and bad, was meant to be.

I started working as a CNA in a nursing home near the Fort Lewis army base, and enrolled in classes at Pacific Lutheran University.

To bare my soul to a man and have him do the same in return made our connection feel out of this world. It was upsetting to me that at one point he had shared a dream he had had when he was very young, that he would die in a war.

We had our ups and downs in the relationship. Before he left for Iraq, we actually had a big argument. Our relationship took a downturn right before he deployed again. Beginning in 2003, we were told he was going to deploy later in the year. They deployed early in November. It was November 23, 2003, when Joe called me from Afghanistan to tell me he had given his life back to Christ and truly believed in God again.

His unit was in the country barely a month when the Strykers rolled over into the canal in Ad Duluiyah, Iraq—December 8, 2003. Sergeant Bridges and Specialist Wesley died instantly. Joe's sling for his weapon caught on something inside the Stryker, trapping him under the water and he drowned.

We had three years together total; for two of them, we were married.

I had a dream, or really a waking vision, of Joe the night he died in Iraq. It was right before I received word of his death. In the dream Joe came to me. It was more like an encounter than a dream; it was so incredibly powerful and real.

He was wearing his BDUs (battle dress uniform, basically fatigues). We hugged each other, held each other, and communicated; so powerful and real. I was telling him I was sorry for my part in everything that went wrong in our relationship and asked him to forgive me. I understood why I felt he hurt me, and knew he didn't mean to hurt me, and that I loved him and always would.

He let me know that he understood too, and forgave me too. He said, "We cannot really blame ourselves for this disruption. I'm okay, and I love you more than anything."

This changed everything inside of me toward Joe concerning the argument we had before he deployed. It was extremely comforting and healing.

The knock on the door came at 1 a.m., notifying me he had died in the accident. That's when I learned he had died. Real life seemed to intertwine with the spiritual life. I could not believe it, yet I was forced to believe that his dreams as a teenager came true; he did die in war, after all.

I felt like the reality of the world I had known had split and shifted. I felt God's hand in all of it. He came to me at the times I was in the deepest grief, and again in dreams, always comforting me. When Joe's personal items came back from Iraq, months and months later, I found a song he had written. He had always written songs, but this song was dedicated to God. It was dated November 23, 2003, the same day he had called me from Afghanistan to tell me he had given his life back to Christ and truly believed in God again.

Baby, It's You

These were the words I found for the song in his notebook:

WORTHY

This is just how I worship
Singing praise you are worthy
I know I could never sing enough
Praise that you are so worthy
You are my Lord
You are my everything
Jesus hold me close now
Closer than I dreamed I could be
You took an unworthy being
Made me clean and made me worthy
Your word is true
Like your worth is
I love you Lord Jesus
Jesus you are everything
Everything to this world of mine
And this world needs you
Your worth and love
Has No End!

—Joe Blickenstaff, Nov 2003

There were other messages from Joe after he died. Before he left, he loved to play a song for me and light candles. The song is called "Black," by Pearl Jam. Now, I can often see him, feel him, and smell his cologne when I hear this song, and I'm flooded with emotion.

One of Joe's friends, Jesse, sent a message to me. He was in a different Stryker unit when the two Strykers fell into the canal. Jesse told me, "Joe came to me twice in an identical dream. I was in a convenience store or gas station buying snacks when Joe came up to me. I felt a wave of relief as I tried to tell him we all thought he died. But here he was, and we were wrong; that is what I felt. Then I realized he was drenched and unresponsive and had a sad look on his face. Then I woke up."

I felt Joe came to Jesse to assure him he was still with him.

Joe came to his stepdad also. He told me, "I remember a dream right after Joe died. I saw Joe smiling, flying around ten thousand miles an hour, swimming with dolphins, and his life was so free and alive; the weight was off his shoulders. I loved the dream. It was like Joe's soul was entering the water and joining each bigger and bigger body of water, until he made it to the ocean—the universal consciousness."

I think of Joe when I hear Peter Gabriel sing the words from "Washing of the Water": "River, river ... living river, carry me on to the place I come from."

James and Sarah

(Lt. Col. James J. Walton, as told by his wife, Sarah)

"I see friends shaking hands,
Sayin', how do you do;
They're really sayin', I love you."

—Louis Armstrong

James (Jim) Walton and I danced to the music of Louis Armstrong's song at our June wedding. It was held in an outdoor garden in Richmond, Virginia. Jim was thirty-seven; I was thirty-five.

We had been married just shy of four years when Jim's life ended, KIA in Afghanistan. He was an avid skydiver. He logged thousands of jumps and he loved CREW, which is where skydivers make formations together with their canopies open.

It was very hot the day of Jim's burial in Arlington National Cemetery. I was seated as everyone joined us at the gravesite. I was feeling the heat when all of sudden, I looked up and noticed a blue sky with only a few puffy clouds. I thought, *Boy, this is beautiful skydiving weather. Jim would be skydiving right now!* At that precise moment, I felt the coolest breeze shower across my face. It was so refreshing and almost impossible to believe it could happen on such a still, humid day. I felt as if Jim was touching me, letting me know that he appreciated me thinking of skydiving. I know he is a skydiving fool in heaven!

Jim was a gentleman. He taught me lots of things about how a gentleman is supposed to behave: how to escort a lady, how to walk on the outside of a lady, how to engage with strangers and make new friends. He was the consummate gentleman, and he became even more polished at West Point. It was not too long after Jim's death when I had a dream, or more like a visit.

In it, Jim took me to a tailor to get his uniform fitted for my body. And then we had lessons, such as walking down sidewalks. I was in a sad place at that time in my life and felt like I could not handle everything. I know this was Jim's way of telling me that I am capable and know just as much as he did. I felt stronger after that dream, but of course I still missed him terribly.

I had another dream with Jim. The dream seemed to come at another time in my life when I felt I was floundering. It's hard to face the long years ahead of me sometimes, and this dream had special meaning.

Jim and I were on a lake or an ocean. We were swimming underwater together. Jim was a master swimmer, a member of the diving team at West Point. He could swim like a dolphin. We were inside a sunken ship underwater and, even though we could potentially get trapped or never escape, I was not afraid since I was with Jim. He gestured for us to swim farther down, into the lower levels of the ship, where he showed me a way out. I was not afraid at all and swam farther down behind him. The next thing I knew, I was out and swimming to the water's surface. It was a beautiful dream and I missed him so much when I woke up. I think he was trying to encourage me not to be afraid and to keep going.

There have been other times I sense him around. One day I was driving and feeling blue, when Annie Lennox's song, one of Jim's favorites, came on the radio, "A Thousand Beautiful Things." As I listened to the lyrics, I saw a flock of birds flying above me; it was quite beautiful. I truly felt that Jim was trying to communicate with me. He wanted me to remember the beautiful side of life. It moved me so much that I still think of that uplifting moment when I hear those words.

Baby, It's You

A friend, Julian, was one of Jim's soldiers during his tour of Iraq. They were close buddies, and Julian had a difficult time with Jim's passing. It was the Christmas after Jim's death; Julian was shopping at a very busy mall. He was having a rough time that day. He thought he saw a man who looked exactly like Jim walking past. Julian stopped in his tracks. The man quickly was lost in the crowd. Julian's focus shifted to the ground where he saw a silver object, and he bent down to pick it up.

Coins are a big deal in the military, and Jim was always interested in them. This one was in the shape of a coin, but it was different—simple and plain silver. It had an image of an angel on one side. Julian knew right away this was meant for him to pick up. Julian flipped the coin over and the name *James* was on it. Julian was blown away and was so moved that he had to leave the mall. He went to his car and tried not to cry. Then a song came on the radio that was special to their time in Iraq, and Julian knew for sure that Jim was checking on him. Sadly, we could not identify the song that came on the radio. Julian was killed in a car accident in February 2013.

If you can sign up for angel duty in heaven, I know Jim went straight to that line to serve. Julian is with him too.

We do know another song that was important to James. It might have been "If You Are Reading This" by Tim McGraw:

*"And war was just a game
We played when we were kids."*

—Tim McGraw

Jim was very patriotic and loved our national anthem. Whenever I hear it, I stop, put my hand over my heart and feel close to Jim.

The Star Spangled Banner

Oh, say can you see by the dawn's early light

What so proudly we hailed at the twilight's last gleaming?

Whose broad stripes and bright stars through the perilous fight,

O'er the ramparts we watched were so gallantly streaming?

And the rocket's red glare, the bombs bursting in air

Gave proof through the night that our flag was still there

Oh say does that Star Spangled Banner yet wave

O'er the Land of the Free

and the Home of the Brave?

—Francis Scott Key

Addison and His Granddaughter, Lila

(Sgt. Addison Smith, as told by his granddaughter Lila)

*"We'll meet again
Don't know where, don't know when ..."*

—Vera Lynn

[NOTE: Names have been changed to protect identities. —MM]

I was in my late thirties, the mother of two children, when I had this unusual experience meeting my grandfather Addison. He was a veteran of WWII, and when I was very young, we would spend time together in the garden. We especially loved picking strawberries. It was a trying time in my life when my grandfather made an appearance from the other side.

My son was eight years old and was playing with friends in the yard when he was accidentally shot in the eye with a BB gun. It was a severe injury that caused permanent damage to his retina, completely losing sight in one eye. I was in a horrible place in my life, with little hope.

One sunny day after the accident, despite how horrible I felt about life at the moment, I went outside to my garden where I sensed an overwhelming fragrance of fresh strawberries everywhere. I saw my grandfather actually appear in my garden. He was standing in full army uniform. He showed me how he had fought in the war. I heard battle sounds, and he kept showing me his array of helmets, the old helmets, heavy-made of metal and used for more than protective head gear.

He showed me how he used his helmet to dredge through heavy water and trees. There were marshes and water that came up to his knees. I could feel the heaviness of the packs the soldiers were carrying, much like the weight I was feeling over my son's burden of being hit by the BB gun. Grandpa was pulling me out of the sunken marsh; I could see the trees and bushes around the bend. I got a very cold feeling, and then I could feel my grandpa pull me out of the marsh. It was as if he were taking my pain away! It was remarkable and still vivid to this day, many years later.

"Don't know where, don't know when
But I know we will meet again some sunny day."

—Vera Lynn

David and His Mother, Michelle

(Sgt. David W. Johnson, as told by his mother, Michelle)

"Look in my heart
And let love keep us together, whatever."

—Captain and Tennille

(Songwriters, Howard Greenfield / Neil Sedaka)

My son, Sgt. David W. Johnson, was in the National Guard. He had enlisted in the Guard right out of high school and served four years. David was a sweet kid, always kind and loving, who enjoyed the creative energy of cooking. He started working as a cook in Portland, Oregon, when 9/11 happened. David had motorcycle buddies from the first enlistment, and they had some discussions about how the Northwest area could be vulnerable to war. David had a calling to rejoin.

I remember the night he called to tell me he was going back in, I was at the stove making gravy. He was thirty-five years old then. "That is stupid," I thought. It was a gut feeling I could not share with him.

I had my own plant nursery at the time, cultivating medicinal plants especially for naturopaths and alternative medicine. I had to memorize all the Latin names of the plants, and it was second nature to me, as I dove into the work.

David had been in Iraq for about six months, halfway through his commitment. My mom had a terminal illness, so I was about to leave for Albany to deal with her at the nursing home. The night before I left, I was very tired. When I walked up the stairs, I felt like someone was putting a black hood over my head. I fell sideways into the stair wall. David's picture fell off the wall with other family pictures. I went straight to bed, and in my head I heard trains hitting each other like two engines colliding in a big crash.

In the morning, I started to pack up the car. My neighbor and best friend for over thirty years came running into the house to tell me, "You cannot leave for Albany! "

"Why?"

"Randy called me and told me that David has been killed. The army has the wrong address since you moved, and they went to Randy's home." Randy is my other son.

I was dumbfounded and thought she was crazy until the soldiers appeared within minutes at my door. "Sgt. David Johnson was in a convoy in the last Humvee and shot by shrapnel from behind. He was killed on September 25, 2004."

I immediately remembered the night before and my experience of the trains crashing, my disoriented feeling and David's pictures falling off the wall. The time zone would have been about the time of his death—an eleven-hour time difference.

It was difficult for me to move on in the plant business after his death. Even the Latin names of all the plants had disappeared from my brain on this journey. It was strange. I was on a mission to speak against the war and try to let my voice be heard.

Not long after, I was contacted by Cindy Lee Miller Sheehan, an American antiwar activist whose son Casey was killed by enemy action during the Iraq War. I had never been on an airplane before, and I had agreed to protest the war at George Bush's ranch. I felt deeply passionate about it.

Before David had shipped out for Iraq, he convinced me to buy a small MP3 player, and he bought a larger one. I thought I should use his player on the plane; it might make the time go faster. So I went down in the basement where his boxes of items were being stored. I got the player, but I couldn't find the cord. It was nowhere to be found. My husband had another kind of player, but that cord wouldn't work with this system.

The morning I was leaving, the cab arrived at the door. I reached for my bag and found a cord on the back of the chair in the bedroom. My husband did not leave a cord there. The song on the MP3 player was one of David's favorites—Josh Groban's "You Raise Me Up." I know David was with me.

At his service, our daughter picked a song by Ozzie Ozborne, Black Sabbath, "I Will See You on the Other Side." She and David were fans. Every time my daughter comes to see me or there is some momentous occasion, that song comes on the radio momentously.

There were so many things I had to deal with after his death. David was not that organized. I had no idea where to find the papers to sell his car or his motorcycle, but it's as if I was led right to the box in the basement. It was like someone took over for me; I can't explain it. The files were all lined up at the top of a box. Another sign David was here.

My son was a big guy. As I was sitting out on the porch about a year after he died, I could feel a sense of warmth and love all over. It was a peaceful feeling, sweet, like he was right with me.

Probably the strangest connection was when I visited a psychic. She seemed very authentic, not wanting any specific information from me. My mother immediately came through, and I was feeling terrified David would not. Out of the blue, the psychic started laughing and asked, "Do you remember the song 'Love Will Keep Us Together' by Captain and Tennille?"

The psychic added, "David is laughing and pointing at me; he must think I don't know that song from my generation! He just keeps laughing!"

"That's because I can see my son dancing to that song. It comes on the radio and I think of him," I replied.

The messages keep on coming. I will often walk alone in the woods, and out of nowhere I will smell cigarette smoke. He smoked cigarettes. It stinks. No one else is around. It has to be him.

It was a good year and a half after he died when I decided to go back to school and study massage therapy and learn about alternative healing modalities. There was a gal in the class who had unusual psychic abilities. We were all sitting around in a circle. "I have someone trying to talk to me," she said. "The noise is loudest behind that chair. I have a *son* energy here? Would anyone have lost a son?"

I nodded my head.

"He is telling me you had a smile that could light up the night, but he does not see it anymore."

"I am not happy. I am depressed, and maybe David is upset with me for speaking against the war."

"He is so proud of you and he is okay with it. He wants you to be happy and shake off this sadness."

I did feel relieved after hearing this message, that David was okay with my voice. I felt lighter and happier.

We have purchased property in eastern Oregon. We are considering making a contribution to veterans, maybe providing housing, maybe a retreat center. We don't know yet. We know this place is healing, filled with silence and a place of solitude. I can still feel the weight of David's chin on my shoulder and the weight of his arms on my shoulders when he leaned into me for a final hug that last time together. I know it is him.

We are now in a place to feel the sweetness, and we hope to share that feeling with others.

Firefighter Michael and His Mother, Nancy

(Probie firefighter Michael D'Auria, as told by his mother, Nancy)

"You're the queen of my heart;
Your love is like tears from the stars."

—Boyz II Men

Lovin' you is like food to my soul. I am Nancy D'Auria, the mother of probie Michael D'Auria, age twenty-five, a rooky fireman on the force for about nine weeks when the fateful call went out to Engine 40-Ladder 35. Michael was on his way to his second-ever fire, and died on September 11, 2001.

Michael gave me this song on a tape a few years before he died. He brought it over on my birthday and put it on the player and danced with me.

His body was discovered after several months, in January 2002. Although I have not had a visitation dream about Michael, I so wish for one. I did have some unusual connections with him.

Michael had moved back home and was living on Staten Island with me for a year before 9/11. Several months after Michael's body was found, my husband and I took a trip to Florida. While we were driving south, I sensed a distinct fragrance of a man's cologne. It was a sharp oriental and woody fragrance that has notes of mint, coffee, caramel, lavender, and tar. I immediately knew the distinct smell of Angel cologne in the car, the cologne Michael wore when he was alive. Angel, the first perfume created by Thierry Mugler, described as "evoking the emotion of tender childhood memories together with a sense of dreamlike infinity," the cologne Michael chose in his short life.

Michael made a statement to his sister, Christina, several months before September 11: "I know when I die it's going to be in a big way and it's going to change the world."

How right you were, my son. Michael loved getting tattoos, but they each had a very special meaning to him. Saint Michael the Archangel sat on his right shoulder—his protector.

Michael began painting during the last year of his life, something he never tried before. But when he did, he uncovered a talent that amazed people who saw his paintings. In the vision in Daniel 10:13–21, an angel identifies Archangel Michael as the protector of Israel. Daniel refers to Michael as a "prince of the first rank." Later in the vision in Daniel 12:1, Daniel is informed about the role of Michael during the "Time of the End," when there will be "distress such as has not happened from the beginning of nations."

Wikipedia describes Michael the Archangel: "At that time Michael, the great prince who protects your people, will arise."

A friend of Michael's had confided in him that he wanted to be cremated. So I had his remains cremated and buried in a crypt at the Moravian Cemetery in Staten Island. One of Michael's hobbies was cooking. He had attended Culinary School and loved to cook. When Christina, my daughter, visited Michael a short while after his internment, she smelled cookies baking when she approached his crypt. There are no bakeries or establishments near this cemetery. The smell was distinct: freshly baking chocolate chip cookies! Michael loved to bake cookies; this was a pure signal he was connecting with Christina at that time. Christina and I had no doubt it was Michael.

Christina's children were at the house a few years after Michael's death. They were two and half years old and had not met Uncle Michael; they were born after his passing. Vanessa, the older one, was playing hide-and-seek in Grandma's living room. Christina asked them what they were doing, and Vanessa said, "We're playing hide-and-seek with Uncle Michael."

Christina kept a sign in her kitchen that was filled with the words we were told Michael said before he died: Live, Love and Laugh. When Vanessa was just a toddler she pointed to the sign. She was very little and would put her arms around someone and follow this person around the room. When Christina asked, the child said, "It's Uncle Michael; he is following me!"

Danial and Melany

(Army Master Sgt. Danial Adams, as told by his wife, Melany)

"What have we found?
The same old fears.
Wish you were here."

—Pink Floyd

Danial and I met one night at a nightclub in Columbus, Georgia, in 1996. I was going through a divorce and had two small boys under the age of five years old, John and Jeffrey. As you can imagine, I didn't get out much. On the night I met Dan, a friend had convinced me to go out and have a few drinks with her and relax. I just wanted to have a good time with my friend and had no plan on meeting anyone. Men were the last thing on my mind!

Dan at the time was in Ranger Battalion, stationed at Fort Benning. Halfway through the evening, Dan kept asking me if I wanted to dance; I kept politely refusing, but he was very persistent. Finally, after about the tenth time, I said, "If I dance with you, will you leave me alone?"

With a big smile, he nodded. "Yes! Hold on!"

He vanished for a few minutes. After returning, he said, "Whatever the DJ plays next, we will dance to the song!"

I had no idea at the time that he had requested the song. It was "Erotic City" by Prince. I looked at him with a "Really?" kind of look, he smiled and said, "Well, let's dance, Melany."

I was wondering what this guy was thinking. Does he think I'm going home with him? Because I'm not.

He was wearing beige corduroy pants and a Wonder Bread hat that was signed by all the bartenders in Buckhead, Atlanta. He had a booger in his left nostril and slobbered from being so hammered. I can still see it clearly.

As we danced he introduced himself in a slurred voice, "My name is Dan, Dan Adams."

[86]

I decided to be a smart-ass and answered, "Oh, like the beer."

This backfired on me. He chuckled under his breath and looked at me with a huge smile, his eyebrows raised, as he said, "No, dumb ass, that's *Sam* Adams."

I could not contain myself and busted out laughing. As we both laughed about it, it totally broke the ice and, to the day he died, we still laughed about it.

Later that night, after the club closed, we all went to Denny's to eat, and Dan asked me for my phone number. I'm not sure why I gave it to him, probably since at the time he was not someone I would normally go for. I gave my number to him with no hesitation, and in doing so, it proved to be one of the best things I have ever done in my life.

Dan's personality and smile were contagious. He was the type of person who made you laugh; he always had a smile on his face. He could insult you with a smile and you'd agree with him and smile back. Dan was a prankster and loved to make people laugh. He could diffuse any situation with humor. He was just an extraordinary man.

We always had fun, no matter what we were doing. We had lots of get-togethers and bonfires at the house. As long as we were together, everything was perfect. I finally got my divorce, which took two years, and as soon as the final judgment arrived in the mail, on March 12, 1998, Dan said, "Let's go."

"Go where?"

"We are going to get married."

I laughed, "You got it, Hot Stuff."

The next day (by the way, Friday, March the 13th), we went to the justice of the peace and were married. Our boys were very young when we met. Soon after we married, the boys asked him, "Will you be our daddy?"

"You are already my boys and nothing will ever change that," he said, adding, "and if you two still feel that way in two years, I will adopt you." Two years later, that's exactly what they did, and their dad made it official. Dan was an amazing person, and he touched the lives of everyone he has ever come in contact with. He was the best family man!

He deployed to Iraq once and Afghanistan four times.

He eventually became a Special Forces team sergeant and got his own team a few months prior to leaving. This is what he always dreamed of doing, taking his men to combat. He knew I was growing tired of him being gone, and we had a discussion before he left. He said to me, "Babe, I know I've been gone a lot, and if you want me to, I will take another job that will keep me home for a few years."

I knew that becoming a team sergeant and taking a team down range was what he always wanted. Reluctantly I told him, "Go ahead, Punkin. I've waited for you this long, I can wait a little longer."

Our plan was to move to Colorado after he got back from this deployment with his guys and after he finished his two years as a team sergeant. Or he would take a job at Fort Bragg within the Special Forces community where he could be home for a few years.

For a while I blamed myself; I thought if had I been selfish and told him, "No, I don't want you to take the team; I want you to stay home," maybe he would still be here with us.

I know the answer is *No, he would have died a different way, maybe a horrible accident.* I know he would not have wanted to leave this earth any other way than the way he did—defending our country, fighting for what he believed in, and being there for his men. Dan's motto was "My Family, My Country, My Honor." My oldest son, John, has MFMCMH tattooed on his arm as a tribute to his father.

A week and a half prior to his final deployment to Afghanistan, I had a vision and could not get it out of my head. It was vivid, and I knew it was not normal. I was in the bedroom at Dan's computer desk writing a eulogy. After Dan died, I was asked to write something for the service and I found myself in the same situation as the dream, in his office chair writing the words. I know now that it was someone from above warning me, to prepare me of what was to come.

I told Dan about the dream while we were in the bathroom one morning, three days before he left, and he assured me, "I am going to be okay, Baby, and this is going to be the last time I deploy."

"I love you, Baby, I love you, and I am so thankful for you. I want to be a better person because of you."

We said some other things to each other that needed to be said and kissed and hugged many, many times in the bathroom. "I love you, I love you," he told me many times.

Again, it was like someone was forcing me to say these things as if I wasn't going to see him again, and that's how I felt before I told Dan what I was seeing. After we said everything we needed to say, we went over again what we wanted for the other if either of us ever died. We did this every time before a deployment. He would always give me confidence. "I am going to be okay, and you are much stronger than you think."

The vision and the strong feeling went away. It felt like BAM! You need to say this! Once I said it, everything went away and my thoughts were calm again. My younger son, age eighteen, was having nightmares about death and dying about a month before Dan deployed. I had to calm him down, dismiss his fear, and reassure him that Dan would be okay. Little did we know his fear was justified.

My son is very intuitive, and has been since he was quite young. A few days after Dan was deployed, he again had nightmares of Dan's death and dying. It was September 2011, and we were talking on Skype and had made a date to talk at a particular time the next day. When I checked the next day, Dan wasn't on line.

I was just finishing an application when I pushed the submit button and heard someone knock at the door at 11 p.m. It was two soldiers who arrived to notify me of his death.

"He was shot," the soldier told me. I later found out he had been shot ten times, no pain, instant death. Not even a moment to reach for his medic bag. He died September 13 leading a team of twelve members in what military officials described as an intense firefight in central eastern Afghanistan. He was thirty-five years old.

The soldiers asked me to go Dover, so I could meet him plane side as he touched down on American soil. I started crying hysterically and ran to our bedroom.

"Dan, I need a sign you are still with me, anything. I need this to be a strong sign, Dan." I kept crying and crying. Immediately, after calling out to him again, I felt a wave of total calm and peacefulness. I fell deeply asleep. When I awoke, I was sure I had been asleep for hours and missed the plane. It had been only ten minutes; I was so calm, it seemed almost surreal.

I looked at my watch again; it had stopped at the moment I asked Dan for a sign he was still with me. It was Dan answering my call out!

Dan was killed eleven days after arriving in Afghanistan for his fifth deployment. After he was killed, I was asked if I wanted to write something for his service. I said, "No, I can't do it. I can't handle that."

But one day before his service, I felt another strong urge, like I had when he and I were standing in the bathroom before he left. I felt like I needed to tell him how much I loved him. I didn't realize until days after, that I found myself in the same situation as in my dream. I was in our room at the same computer desk, crying as I wrote his eulogy. I honestly think I was being warned, to prepare myself for what was to come by someone who had already passed. Who? I don't know.

I felt that same calm several months later. I was inside the department of motor vehicles, signing off his car, and I could smell so clearly a certain smell that army men have. "You are here, Dan. I know this is you, Dan."

I was sitting down, and it was as if he was standing behind me. I felt like he was right behind me, wrapping his arm around my right side. I felt a tingling from my right shoulder blade as if he was there giving me a hug.

Almost a year after he was gone, I went to Germany to visit his team. Dan was master sergeant; my two oldest sons were stateside for a get-together while I was gone. One of the kids told me how he was standing next to the sink talking to someone, but no one answered him. He later shared it was Dan. He saw him clearly.

About a month after Dan died, my daughter, Skye, thirteen years of age (2011) said she saw Dan in the hallway. "Dad had his black socks on and his black army workout shorts, and he turned around and smiled at me, Mom. I knew he was happy, Mom."

I feel comfort knowing Dan is with us. No doubt he answered my calls, and since I had those experiences, the grief I carry has been lightened.

My son John wanted to follow in his dad's footsteps and was going to join the army before Dan was killed, but didn't join until after. He did say that while he was in basic training, he was ready to quit a few times. Then he heard his dad in his head saying, "You can do it, you can do it, don't give up."

I feel comfort knowing Dan is with us and watching over us. He answers my calls; he gives me signs. I have been able to be strong for myself and our children.

I am no longer afraid to die. From the experience my whole family has had, I know there is life after death and I will see him again. I know that we all will see *them* again, and they will be there to take us home when it's our time. Knowing this has made our hearts heal and our souls grow.

Stand with Me

I know you eat at our table with us,
stand behind me at the counter.
I can smell you in the moment.
Whispers of love melt into my ear.
Your motto now echoes in our hearts
All in the name of your oath:
My Family, My Country, My Honor.
—Maureen McGill

Michael and Jessica

(Capt. Michael Braden, as told by his wife, Jessica)

*"They [angels] come to you and me in our darkest hours
To show us how to live, to teach us how to give ..."*

—Alabama

I met my husband, Michael, in the laundry room of our college dorm at Slippery Rock University of Pennsylvania on September 11, 2000. He carried my underwear back to the room for me! Guess you can say it was an "intimate" first meeting. I was a second-year social work major and Michael was a second-year ROTC cadet majoring in information systems management. We immediately hit it off and quickly fell in love.

We dated the remainder of our college days. When we graduated in 2003, we decided to take a break and see where fate would take us. Michael had just been commissioned as a second lieutenant in the Army Signal Corps; I went on to get my master's in social work. We never lost contact and knew there was still something there.

Sadly, Michael discovered a couple of years later that he had a seizure condition. In October 2005, Michael suffered a seizure in Iraq. I was the first person he called after the incident. He didn't even call his parents first! It was then that I knew we were still in love.

We started flying back and forth to visit each other every few months and talked every single night. Finally, in June 2007, Michael proposed to me. He then shipped off to Korea for a year. He came back safely, and we got married in January 2009 in the most beautiful ceremony imaginable. We pledged our love in front of our family and friends on the coldest day in Pittsburgh in over twenty years. We went on the honeymoon of a lifetime to Jamaica, and when we came back, we moved to Fort Riley, Kansas.

We began our married life.

Right before our first anniversary, he was deployed to Basra, Iraq, for a year. We spoke every single day, and we knew we were ready to start our family. We had decided to adopt our first child. This became a challenge from the start, with seventeen failed matching opportunities.

Our son, James, was finally placed with us on May 20, 2011. He was twenty-one months old. Our dreams had come true! The first photo we took of James showed him playing with a little metal "waste management" truck in a quiet carpeted room.

Shortly after the adoption, Michael found out he would be deploying to Afghanistan. Over the next year, we endured Michael working seven days a week, twelve to fourteen hours a day. Then, on August 16, we learned that our adoption was being contested by the birth father. Between the stress of the court hearings and the deployment prep, that was the most stressful time of our lives. We finally were able to finalize our adoption on our third wedding anniversary on January 17, 2012.

The next three months were very stressful. Michael was getting ready to ship off to Afghanistan and I was getting ready to be a single mom for a year. Soon after Michael deployed at the beginning of April, I had a bad gut feeling. I can't explain it. Something felt really awful.

On April 18, 2012, I woke up and immediately checked my e-mail, as I normally did, expecting my daily "Hey I'm alive and safe" message that Michael promised me he would send. When I didn't get the e-mail that day, I didn't think too much of it. I thought maybe he had been busy. But, I could not shake the feeling that something really bad had happened. I continued to e-mail him and tried to call him, with no luck. At lunchtime, two of my friends started calling me. They were asking if I had heard from Michael because they hadn't heard from their husbands.

"No, I haven't heard from him."

I was working an hour from where we were living, so by the time I picked up my son and grabbed some fast-food take-out, we finally arrived home at 6:40 p.m. At 6:47, we were sitting at the table eating our chicken nuggets and watching the *Golden Girls* when there was a knock at the door. I was notified of Michael's death. Captain Michael

Braden had passed away in his sleep from a fatal seizure, four months after we adopted little James.

To make matters more difficult, a few months later a very close friend of mine from high school, Ashlee, passed away from cardiac arrest due to a congenital heart defect. She was tall and pretty, with long wavy, ginger-red hair, and brown eyes. She had the smile of an angel and a heart of gold, and only wanted to please people and be happy.

Ashlee and I were close friends and knew each other from marching band in high school. I was devastated because the day of Ashlee's viewing, there was a major accident on the turnpike and I had to turn the car around. I could not attend the service.

I had never had the honor of meeting Ashlee's husband, Mike, but I knew at least I had to reach out to this young widower and offer my support. I sent him a Facebook message, and about a week later he messaged me back. Mike said he was not *into* Facebook, but wanted to thank all those who offered support to him.

We started out as grief buddies, but soon discovered we had much more in common. We were both living in Pittsburgh at the time. Our friendship continued. He had never met my Michael.

"I think I really like you. I want to take you out on a date," Mike said. It was my birthday, and I was a bit apprehensive. This was only three months after losing Ashlee, and nine months after I lost Michael.

My answer: "We are adults here, both thirty-one years old. Let's just go out and have a pizza or something!" I thought he was handsome, but romantic interest was not in the picture; we were a couple of grieving spouses.

We had a few things in common. Mike and Ashlee were also going through the adoption process like us, but Ashlee died before a baby came into their lives. Mike told me, "Ashlee had this heart condition and faced death three times when she almost died on the table each time."

He shared with me that after Ashlee's third near-death experience, she told him that her friend Jessica's (me) husband had died in the war in Afghanistan. I had not posted anything about Michael's death anywhere. He had died only one week before she made that statement. Ashlee was one of the first friends to reach out to me after my husband's death. We think Ashlee saw Michael on the other side in one of her near-death experiences! How could she know?

Within a few months, Mike and I had fallen deeply in love and decided to spend time together.

We are both convinced we get messages from our sweeties. Probably one of the first connections is when Mike saw a picture I posted on Facebook of our newly adopted twenty-one-month-old baby James, playing with that waste management truck. Mike was dumbfounded when he saw the photo; he works for a waste management firm in Pennsylvania. The truck was the same color. It seemed too coincidental.

Another strange occurrence happened on the day Michael died in Afghanistan from a fatal seizure on April 18. The army was not sure how long he had been dead. They think he actually died in the late hours of April 17. Mike shared with me a strange occurrence they had with their Yorkshire puppy that day. It was late in the evening, and time for bed. "Daisy is usually very quiet, but on that night of April 17, the dog went ballistic for about a half hour. It was the exact same time the officials were discovering Michael's body in Afghanistan." Mike had written down the time because it was his birthday and later realized the significance.

Michael and Ashlee always come to us in our dreams. Usually they come to us together and will either be smiling at us or sometimes have a message for us like, "It's okay."

The other morning Mike shared with me. "Your dead husband came to me in a dream last night. Michael, James, and I were standing on a tarmac. We hugged, and Michael said, 'It's okay.' Then he boarded a plane and it exploded."

Unbeknown to Mike, on the exact same night I had a dream about his Ashlee. (In real life Ashlee was religious, a devout Methodist. I was Presbyterian like her husband, Mike.) In the dream, I was walking down the aisle in my wedding dress and the song "Angels Among Us" by Alabama was playing. Both of our families were there. Ashlee was the officiating pastor who was marrying us, and she was smiling. I know she was giving us her blessing. We think it is divine intervention that we both had a dream about them on the same night!

We have an October wedding date planned. As I think back, there is a sign I cannot help but remember now. When Ashlee and I were in high school, our band took a trip to Disneyland. We ended up getting stuck on the ride, "It's a Small World." It is a small world here too.

Mike and I hooked up, and it took two people to die before we were destined to be together. It is like the opposite of the film *The Notebook*! Destiny, I guess.

James and Lisa

(L.Cpl. James Alvarez, as told by his wife, Lisa)

*"That God blessed the broken road
That led me straight to you."*

—Rascal Flatts

I met L.Cpl. James Gideon Alvarez III when we were kids. I was sixteen, a junior in high school, and he was thirteen in middle school. We knew each other, growing up in the same neighborhood, living five minutes from each other. We didn't really connect closely until much later. I was twenty-two, he was nineteen. I was actually dating his best friend's brother for a while. We met up at a New Year's Eve 2001 party. The party was festive. I was wearing white with a black chiffon flowy long overshirt, and he was wearing a bright red shirt. He had short hair and pretty greenish-blue eyes. We talked, partied, and our love began. We dated for five years, while James worked for his dad's vacuum and appliance store. He wanted to serve his country and

fight for what he believed in so he chose to join the Marine Corps in January 2006. He wrote me numerous love letters from boot camp and those few and far between phone calls filled with silences. On August 12, 2006, eight months later we got married, and I became Lisa Alvarez.

Our wedding was loud with lots of love in the room. He wore his dress blues, and I wore a long white dress. When the wedding party was introduced we danced out, to the song "Me and My Gang," another song by Rascal Flatts. For hours we danced to different sounds, from country, to oldies, to dance/booty music.

Our daughter, Madison, was born January 2, 2007, and our son, Tyler, was born December 7, 2012. We used to enjoy playing pool together and watching football games. I called him *James* and *Honey*; he called me *Babe*. James had smooth skin, a sweet nose, and a serious look.

He was a veteran of the Iraq War, and the war took its toll on him. Upon his return, he battled depression and PTSD. He was twenty-nine years old when he took his life on March 20, 2013. Do I know it was the destruction, seeing the dead bodies, the loss of life, being shot at, being attacked and ambushed, receiving mortar or rocket fire, knowing someone was killed or seriously injured, visions of explosions, innocent loss of lives that sent him over the edge? Yes, I know it was all of the above. We never talked about what happened and what he saw over there. It was a pact we made before he left. I would never ask ... and he would never tell. He definitely wasn't the same person when he came back.

I've had a few experiences with "signs" after losing my husband, James, to suicide last year. The first one happened after I woke up the morning after. My black tank top was sitting on the bathroom counter on his side, and I saw a yellow ribbon design made out of yellow string. Yellow is used for the ribbons to support the troops and also suicide awareness. I own nothing that is yellow.

The second sign was about six to nine months after he passed. I was lying in bed and could smell a distinct mixture of his cologne, Gucci Envy, and Marlboro Red cigarettes. There he was! I could sense he was there.

We both loved to watch two TV shows, *The Good Wife* and *The Vampire Diaries*, which were scheduled at the exact time. We had this DVR device with our cable company that would record both shows. It was about six to nine months after he passed, and I was alone in the house. I watched on our bedroom TV *The Good Wife*, and when I went to delete the program, the TV read, "You cannot delete the show because it is being watched in another room." It was James. There are other times when I will hear a knock at the door, and no one is there. You can think whatever you want, but my gut tells me it is him.

Tyler was three and a half months old when James died, and I had put him to bed in the crib. There was a fan with a light fixture in the middle. I shut the light off and the fan, but when I went back up fifteen minutes later to check on him, the light was back on. I shouted out, "What are you doing to me? Why are you turning the light on?" Again, my gut knew it was James.

I had not heard our song, "Bless the Broken Road," until Mother's Day, a few months after he died, May 2013. I walked into a restaurant with my family for our special dinner, and the song was playing over the speakers as we were seated. I had no doubt he was with us.

The one message that hit me the most happened in June 2014, a year after his death. I was visiting family in Florida and our daughter, age seven, wrote a note to my brother-in-law on their refrigerator saying she loved him. She wrote it like this: *"I ove you."* That is the same way my husband ended his suicide note: *"I ove you Lisa."* My sister was having a baby the next day, so I think it was his way of letting me know he was with us. My daughter is seven and doesn't know that her daddy ended his life so she has never seen the note. It is locked in my safe.

*"I'd like to have the time I lost
And give it back to you."*

—Rascal Flatts

Hero of 9/11

(A 9/11 hero, as told by his friend)

"In your heart, in your mind
I'll stay with you for all of time."

—The Calling

[NOTE: Names have been changed to protect identities. —MM]

New York was just waking up again, nine days after 9/11/2001, and some movement in the streets had begun. It could have been me in those Towers. After high school, I went to work at Cantor Fitzgerald, a financial services firm located in the World Trade Center on the 105th floor of the Twin Towers. I quit in 1993 after the first bombings.

I knew many of the company members who were killed in that office on 9/11. There was a close friend, Vinny; I knew him from childhood. We went all through school together since kindergarten. We grew up in the same neighborhood. Vinny was a football player, and I was a cheerleader in high school. Vinny was close to my family. We remained pals, attending neighborhood parties over the years. He stayed with the company after I resigned. He was married only two months when his life was taken. He was the youngest in that office to leave this world. I picked the song "Wherever You Will Go" for Vinny's wife. *"I'll stay with you for all of time."*

I was returning from my college in Manhattan eight days after the planes hit. I was walking along Seventh Avenue near Fashion Avenue to catch the train from school during the noon hour. The sun was bright and the street was crowded, but the sun kept beating on my face. My dad was a fireman in the city on 9/11; so many people still were missing. My dad and his friends carried Vinny's picture in hope someone had seen him. I was hoping in my heart, people were still going to be found alive. Pedestrians were crying as they walked past me. Families posted pictures of missing loved ones along the buildings, in hope they would be found.

They found Vinny's watch, but they never found his body.

I was not even thinking specifically of Vinny on that day as I walked to the train. When I felt an arm slide around my back and pull me close, I thought it was a stranger and got scared, but no one was there! I got a rush through my whole body. Then I heard Vinny's voice so clearly whisper in my ear, "I'm fine, I'm fine." I knew at that moment he was okay. I got this rush of a feeling.

"Everything's going to be all right. Take care of our friends, I love you," Vinny said.

I looked up and now I could see his face clearly. "I know I will take care of them, and I love you too," I told him.

He appeared as he was when I knew him, tall, good looking, muscular, in his late twenties, with a mustache. I would describe seeing a translucent image of him. We took about seven steps together. I felt lighter afterward, supported.

People were staring at me because my arm was in the air, holding his waist, and I was telling the sky, *I love you too.* I just cried and cried. He was an awesome person and friend. I'm glad he stopped by to see me. It was very comforting and real.

Baby, It's You

Over and Over

Into dust they disappeared

Moment to moment

Photos of faces imprinted on every sidewalk

They walk with us now in dreams

In visions, in smells

Never to be forgotten

Only to be remembered

Over and over

Year after year

Day after day.

—Maureen McGill

Joseph and Ashley

(Army Spec Joseph A. Richardson as told by his wife Ashley)

"The world's a roller coaster... "

—Incubus

Joey and I met during his first tour in Iraq, and we started talking on Facebook; we had the same best friend in common. I didn't know they were best pals! I found out from Joey. He was an athletic guy, loved cross-country and golf. He was even a member of the Future Farmers of America. We talked for five months during his deployment and started talking again when he came home. We started dating October 4, 2010; one month later on November 5, 2010, we got married. We didn't tell anyone except his mom and my grandma. We went to the courthouse and signed our marriage license. The only justice of the peace in town who could marry us also owned a pawn shop, so we got married in a pawn shop in Arkansas, Haha! That's my absolute favorite story. Afterwards we drove to my brother's football

game and hung out at my parent's house. We waited three weeks before we broke the news to my parents. They found out when they read my driver's license. Joey was the best person; he was so genuine and caring. He had a one-of-a-kind sense of humor, and he made everyone laugh.

Joey left for Afghanistan on Mother's Day 2012; it was only a nine month deployment. He laughed at me the whole way to the post because I was crying. Once we stepped out of the car, he looked at me and said, "Are you all right?"

I started bawling and buried my face in his chest. He didn't look back at me when he had to leave. My mom said he had tears in his eyes. We Skyped almost every day and sometimes two times, which I am very grateful for. Joey was going to miss our second anniversary because he was on a weeklong mission. It was 6:30 a.m. the day of our anniversary when I got a call; it was Joey! His infantry training officer let him call me from the satellite phone. It made my whole day. On November 16, 2012, eleven days after our anniversary, my life was forever changed. At 3:42 p.m. Friday, November 16, I got a knock on my door. I didn't think anything about it until I opened the door and there they were. Two officers in dress blues were standing there. I backed away from the door, thinking he was really injured. I kept saying, "Okay, we are about to go to Germany?"

The army had briefed us that may happen. When they replied, "Mrs. Richardson…," I knew we were not going to Germany. "There was an extensive explosion followed by small arms fire and Specialist Joseph was separated from the group and died of his injuries." "NO!" I kept shaking my head. "You wear gear to protect you, and that isn't possible. What happened? Was he alone? Did he leave any messages for someone to tell me? Did he die alone? Was he in pain? Was he scared?" All these were questions nobody could answer. I called my dad first and was crying hysterically and said, "Pick me up right now!" "What's wrong?" "Joey's not coming home!" After that my phone was blowing up from family and friends, and I couldn't do anything. It was the most devastating day of my life. I became a 22-year-old widow. I barely grasped what all my marriage was, and I was just getting into the role of a wife. Becoming a widow is nothing you can prepare for. It's been almost two years and I still can't grasp the concept. I run away from this subject as much as I possibly can. If you talk about it, that makes it real, and I'm not ready for it to be real. Joey was killed by an IED.

The night before I knew he was killed I had a dream: "I was cutting a man's hair, a man who looked like Joey but he wasn't Joey. I kept flirting with him in my dream. While I was cutting his hair, I couldn't get one side of his hair to match the other side, and it wouldn't work. Joey's damage was all on the right side of his body and that made me think the man in my dream was Joey. I kept trying to fix the one side to match the other side, and I couldn't fix it." The day after his death, I could feel him so strongly. I could feel him all around me, and it is the only time I have felt peace. No emotion just peace. He was everywhere. I talked to him so much. On the plane to Dover, I fell asleep and had a dream that I was messaging him. He said, "It's so big here." I think he was letting me know he was okay and telling me how he is doing now. After we saw him in Dover, we went back to the hotel and I was messaging his best friend, Kyle, telling him I wish I could have been a better wife. "ASHLEY!" I heard my name yelled right after I sent that message. I looked up. My mom, mother-in-law, and sister-in-law were all sitting at the table with me. "Who called out my name?" They all looked at me like I was crazy. I told them that someone just said, "Ashley!" I also saw Joey standing next to me outside the hotel, but when I looked in his direction, he would be gone. Still, I could feel him there with me. I could see a man standing in the corner at the funeral home; it was Joey, in his army blues. I looked again and he was gone; I knew it was Joey.

Another time, I was at my parents asleep on the couch. I remember I was cold. I heard my name. "Ashley!" I opened my eyes and right in front of me, right up at the couch, I saw Joey. I could see his silhouette, his shoulders, his head. He had his arms held out like he was holding a blanket. I felt so comfortable, I closed my eyes, and we went back to sleep so peacefully, like we would if he were home. The casualty officer and I were returning from the funeral; we were at the airport. The power went out at the airport and we couldn't get our bags. The officer swears that was Joey telling me to slow down, and I don't have to do everything in one day. We finally got our bags and headed onto the post.

As we drove past the gate, the officer was changing channels on the radio, and there it was! Joey's ring-tone on my phone was the song, "Wish You Were Here," by Incubus — the exact song that was playing on the radio. I had another dream that Joey said he died, but they fixed him and he's okay now. I said to him, "Babe, you died." "Yeah" he replied. "They took me to the hospital in Afghanistan; they fixed me, and I'm alive." I've had another dream where Joey is at my parent's house, and we are just talking. As I was crying and hugging him, he said, "I have to go now."

My grandma had a dream about Joey. They are talking when Joey said to her, "I have to go now." Grandma said, "Wait Joey! I wanna give you a hug." "No grandma, if you touch me you have to go with me." My mom had a dream about Joey. He told her that he would show her what it really was like where he is. "There is a barn structure over here," he said to my mom. "I have to go now." My mom started following him on the stairs when he said, "Stay, because you cannot follow me." Joey and I had tried to have a baby before he was deployed, but I did not get pregnant. About a year after Joey's death I hooked up with his best friend, Jonathan. We both used each other as a crutch to get through the sorrow. I became pregnant.

I was about five months pregnant when I had this vivid dream of Joey with a message. He was wearing his favorite jeans and plaid shirt. "Go to school and get a degree, and enjoy being a mommy." The fiancé of one of the guys Joey deployed with had a miscarriage. Afterwards, on her due date, she had a dream that Joey was sitting on her couch holding a baby in a blanket. He said, "The baby's hair is getting long and curly." He continued talking about the baby girl they lost.

Lisa, the mother said, "Can I see the baby?" Joey said, "We have to go now." Joey would love to toss change on the floor just about anywhere when we lived together. I have found change in the strangest places now. The other message is the smell of his cologne. I smelled it in our closet. His belongings are not there anymore, but at random times I will open the closet door and the fragrance comes through. Probably the strangest message is at our house. It was the house we were going to settle in after his deployment. I had made a shelf shrine to honor Joey, with his flag and some mementos including a gold letter "J". Randomly the "J" would fall off onto the floor. One day I just shouted out, "Don't do that anymore, Joey." He stopped. I felt like he was at the house. He used to love to tap his finger on the coffee table in a kind of drumming rhythm when we lived together. Randomly, after he died, I would hear the same kind of tapping coming from a stove-pipe area on the ceiling that was completely sealed. I know it was him. I'd hear footsteps in the hallway in the bedroom and bathroom. I'd hear the cabinets banging in back where his stuff was packed. I'd hear knocking on the front side of door and on the inside of the door. At night, I would lock the door and in the morning the door lock would be open. It was frightening. The doorbell would go on and off and kept doing that repeatedly. The messages just keep on coming from him. The last one happened yesterday. I was driving on post and saw a license plate number 479; that was the same area code of Booneville, Arkansas, his hometown. His signs clearly ask me to pay attention. Joey is with me, my Purple Heart guy.

Joseph and Ashley

"Maybe I should hold with care, but my hands are busy in the air..."

—Incubus

William and Maria

(E3 William Bonner, as told by his wife, Maria)

*"It was no accident me finding you
Someone had a hand in it."*

—Tracy Byrd

E3 William Bonner enlisted in the US Navy at sixteen years of age. He served for four years working on aircraft carriers during Vietnam, and served as an assistant to the chaplain. Bill went on with a career after Vietnam, and I met him later in life.

He had retired from his career as a carpet installer when we met at the Nazarene Church in Baker City, Oregon. I was in my late forties, and he was in his early fifties. We were going to church. I had gone into the sanctuary and saw Bill sitting on the front row. He started sharing with me about his family, and we went for coffee … and the rest is history.

"Are you dating anyone?" he asked.

We decided to go for a ride. He jumped in my truck, and we drove to a little café in Baker City. I lived behind the Dairy Queen at the time. He came to my place for coffee, and the conversation continued. Bill invited me the next day for country friend chicken, his favorite food, and we just felt like old souls together.

He loved to listen to music, Elvis, and Christian contemporary music. He also had a wonderful bulldog named Sugar. He enjoyed taking her for her daily walks around town. We dated four months and were married on Christmas Day 2009. It was not easy finding a minister on Christmas, so Bill contacted Gerald, whom he had met during a difficult time in his life; Gerald did street ministry. We had a simple ceremony with a party a few weeks later. I wore a white wedding dress with sequins, spaghetti straps, and a beautiful black shawl with white feathers.

We had some funny times together. We both loved to fish. We decided to go off road to a lake one time and ended up getting stuck in the mud. It was like a comedy movie as we rocked back and forth and repeated the same stuck situation three times in a row!

We were married only two years, living in Union, Oregon, when I woke up first and played a game on the computer. Bill woke up with a bad headache. After he took some medicine, I heard him choking and called 911. He died of a brain aneurysm.

I was holding him when he passed. I tried to get him to come around; I ran to a neighbor, called 911, and ran back to the house. I did the painful stimuli at the bottom of his feet, and he came back around. He sat on the edge of the bed and said his head was killing him. He remained on life support for five days, until I got up from the recliner and said to him, "If you cannot get out of this, you can go Home, you can go be with God and his family members." I told him, "You are the best husband and loving brother." *Father*, I prayed, *we want the peace of God*. Bill passed fifteen minutes later. I was with him till he passed. It was not easy.

The September day of Bill's funeral was chilly. I had arranged for Bill's cousin to play his favorite hymn, Elvis's version of "How Great Thou Art." When his cousin sang it, I could feel Bill there. He sang the same tones as Elvis. During the song, the air turned warm and a feeling of warmth spread all over me. I could feel him; I knew he was there.

After his death I would see heart shapes everywhere. As I walked through the leaves, I saw heart-shaped leaves on the ground. I'd look up and see clouds in the shape of hearts. Every time I saw a heart I knew he had my back. I could feel him.

The other day I was walking toward the chickens in our back area and found feathers everywhere. I picked them up. Feathers in Native American legends are gifts from the Great Spirit.

I have felt him when no one is in the room with me. He has touched my shoulder. I sense him sometimes, like a breeze coming through the room. On one hot, steaming, and humid day, all of a sudden it felt cool; the heat subsided and poof, a cool breeze came through. I felt it was him.

I was living in Oregon two months after his passing and was driving down a country road. I had just attended the Agape church.

The sermon was a bit disturbing to me; the theme was about death. The minister preached, "They go to heaven and they are gone, and one must let your loved one go."

I started to cry when I heard that message and could not stop crying. I was crying from the moment I got into the GMC truck Bill had purchased as a wedding/Christmas gift. I am not letting Bill go! I know he is with me forever.

I proceeded to drive down the road home, crying away and listening to a Christian radio station. On came the country song, "Keeper of the Stars," sung by Tracy Byrd. I pulled over to the side of the road. I could not believe this song came on the radio, not a particularly Christian song, but of the country western genre. It was like peace passes all understanding, like a flood, like a fresh rain, all encompassing, the feeling of peace.

That song has come on a lot since Bill passed away. It comes on the radio randomly and it tears me up. I remember the good times, how God drew us together. It is often twice a month I hear it on the radio. Bill makes this happen from the other side. He puts it on the radio as a sign, and I know he still loves me and is walking in streets of gold. I look forward to joining him. Now, I just can't believe you're still in my life!

"Heaven's smilin' down on me
As I look at you tonight."

—Tracy Byrd

[110]

Shawn and Carrie

(Sgt. Shawn Michael Reilly, as told by his wife, Carrie)

"You makin' me live now, honey ...
You're the best friend
That I ever had."

—Queen

I met my husband, Shawn Michael Reilly, in 2005, online of all places! It was a site called "HOT or NOT," an Internet site where people rate photos. He was deployed to Iraq at the time and spent eight dollars to message me. From that moment on, we talked every day for as long as he was able to. I fell deeply in love with this man and his smart-ass sense of humor. He used to tell me that I was a female version of him. He made funny voices and joked with me all the time.

Shawn would do anything for anyone who needed help. He joined the army when he was eighteen and became an army ranger. He was described as "playing army" when he was a full-fledged ranger. Over the years he loved to watch professional football, loved the outdoors, and was an avid hunter.

His first Iraq deployment was for twelve months, and his second tour was almost eighteen months. He drove a vehicle called the HUSKY, which goes out first in line to find the Improvised Explosive Devices (IEDs). He had several encounters with the explosives and incurred traumatic brain injury and PTSD. He also had injuries to both shoulders. He received a Purple Heart for his injuries.

We were engaged when he was deployed, but we didn't get married until August 18, 2008. He came home in late spring, May or June 2008, and was stationed at Fort Knox, in the Warrior Transition Unit (WTU), which is a unit for injured soldiers.

When we were on leave in Las Vegas, the poor guy was on crutches from his injuries in Iraq. It was 120 degrees outside, my a/c went out in my jeep, and Shawn's poor armpits were raw from walking on crutches. He announced, "Let's get married!" This was the hottest

August day in Vegas, and we ended up at the Little White Wedding Chapel for a drive-thru wedding ceremony! We pulled up to the drive-thru window and got married. Best memory of us together ever!

As a sergeant in the army and also an army ranger, he received numerous awards including that Purple Heart. Shawn's nickname from the boys in his unit was Rangersmurf because of his 5'5" stature. He made everyone laugh with his practical jokes.

He had a total of twenty-three years in the service. PTSD took its toll, and Shawn lost his battle to live at his home. He had always told me he would leave signs for me if the time came for him to leave. The night he died, after I left the hospital I drove home alone. I found a penny on the running boards under the doors of my Jeep. No way would a penny have been able to stay there while I was driving to the hospital in a panic. I picked up the penny, looked up into the night sky, and just smiled. I knew he was with me from that moment on.

After I moved home a month later, I was in the living room. My phone sat on the end table, far from the edge of the table. All of a sudden the phone fell to the floor. There was no way it just fell on its own; I felt it was Shawn.

That was not the only sign I received from Shawn. I was in my room looking at his urn of ashes when I started yelling at him. "I am mad at you for leaving me! You said just tonight, you would never do anything to hurt me!" At that moment, I felt a swirl of cold air all around me. The coolness surrounded me. He was there, in my room. I know it in my heart. It was this feeling of comfort all over me.

Our song together was by Queen, "My Best Friend." He truly was my best friend. I still get pennies from him, but now they come whenever I am really down and the grief is overpowering my thoughts. I know he is still here with me. I can smell him sometimes and feel as if he is kissing my cheek and touching my face like he used to. These signs make me feel so loved by him and so sad at the same time.

Not a day goes by I don't miss that man and his silly antics.

*"I'm happy, happy, happy at home
You're my best friend."*

—Queen

Jason and Jennifer

(Spc. Jason D. Hunt, as told by his wife, Jennifer)

"My love has come along ...
And life is like a song."

—Etta James

I met Jason Hunt in late September 2005 while we were working together at Walmart. We became best friends, but secretly I was in love with him. Turns out he felt the same about me, but was too shy to tell me. He joined the army a few months later and we lost touch.

I ended up getting married to someone else, and he had one child. I was pregnant with my second when my husband walked out on me and left me literally barefoot and pregnant.

On Thanksgiving Day, 2006, I received a text from a weird number and it was Jason. I ended up telling him that I had been in love with him, and he confessed to the same feelings. We were pretty much together ever since. We did have a rough patch while he was deployed, and we broke up for a couple months. Other than that, we had about three and a half years altogether.

We were married on August 22, 2009. I wore a traditional wedding dress, and my aunt and grandmother helped with the wedding. They decorated, and they baked the cake. We had the reception at a banquet hall, which was kind of pricey, and we had a great turnout. Jason's mom made food, and his sister took photos alongside our hired photographer. We danced our first dance to Etta James's version of "At Last." I saved the top of the cake and his boutonniere in our freezer.

A strange thing happened to me on the way to the wedding. I actually got lost—on the way to my own wedding! Everyone was freaking out, but once I got there, I was ready before everyone! I have pictures of Jason pacing and looking worried; he wanted that day to be perfect for me. It was perfect, despite the things that went wrong. We had a DJ, danced a bunch together, and did the traditional money dance where people pay to dance with the bride. It was the happiest day of my life.

I tossed the bouquet and didn't get it very far; it landed in front of everyone, not in anyone's hands. Jason went to get the garter off my leg and was down there a long time, the whole crowd laughed as he fumbled to get that thing off. We had white roses with turquoise tips as our wedding flowers. We wrote our own vows; it was a fun wedding.

I was finishing a class in Oklahoma City two months after the wedding, and we planned to move to Fort Hood, Texas, where Jason had bought a house. Jason was preparing for deployment and was stationed there. Strange things started to happen to me on November 5, 2009. I started to go for a jog, which was something Jason would do, not me! You could not pay me to exercise! I grabbed Jason's iPod and listened to his music, which I normally hate. I played several songs while running, none of which I knew because they were heavy metal (I'm more of a Taylor Swift kind of girl).

I was also listening to the ballads the soldiers sing when they are running during PT, or whatever—the army chants—almost as if I were Jason for a few minutes. It was very weird to me.

I ran over a mile straight, farther than I would ever do, being someone who never exercised. The whole time I was running, it felt as if someone was with me, following me. I was convinced someone was following me. Twelve hours later the dreaded knock on the door happened. At that point I knew Jason was with me. It felt like I was taking on his spirit after he died, his spirit joining with me.

[115]

The worst solo mass shooting ever to take place on a US military base happened that infamous day. The shooter targeted twelve soldiers in uniform and one civilian standing in line for immunizations and medical checks. All were killed. Jason was shot and killed in the back; more than thirty others were wounded. Spc. Jason Dean Hunt was twenty-two years old.

I received the same flowers from our wedding for his funeral, white roses with turquoise tips. Since we had written our own vows, I had both of them framed and placed in the casket with him. I also put the top of our wedding cake in there, along with my bouquet. I have his boutonniere in my freezer. I know Jason was around me the entire time of the funeral. A week and a half later, I felt a hand on my back as I stood to wait for the plane that was carrying his body to land. The hand felt real, human. I know it was Jason comforting me.

I have to remember the fun stuff about Jason. Jason was a prankster. He loved to play jokes on anyone. One joke he played during our short marriage was tossing blankets off me. He thought that was so funny. About two months after his death, I was lying in bed, wide awake, when my blanket came flying off me. I knew he was doing this! It came out of nowhere!

Whenever I went into a store or restaurant, our song, "At Last," came on. I would cry uncontrollably.

Jason was an atheist and I am Christian. He and I had a lot of talks about religion, but he'd always brushed what I said off and didn't really listen. He believed that when you die, you just vanish. Two weeks before he died, we were lying in bed and we started to talk about death. He told me that if anything should happen to him to use the money to buy a house and a car. I shushed him. We then started talking about the whole religious aspect, and he actually listened to what I had to say. He had never done that before.

I asked him, "What if something happened to me and I died? Would you want to never see me again?" He actually started to cry, and that was not like him. He looked like he changed his mind about life after death. It is said that if you die not believing in God that you get an automatic trip to hell. I don't know about that. But if it's true, then I kind of feel like that talk was his saving grace. Who knows what's true until we get there?

There was a lot of upset after his death, but one of my concerns was that he was afraid of death, or he would feel afraid. I've had approximately ten dreams since his death, in which he says pretty much the same thing in all of them. He tells me that he is breaking rules by contacting me and that he could get in trouble. In one dream, he was missing, and everyone thought he was dead, but he was found a week later locked in a box, alive.

I'm in the dream and hear him say very clearly, "I am not scared anymore." It was something I wondered about when he died. He is not scared anymore. This resonates with me now; I know he is okay.

There have been other contacts from Jason. There are many times I can smell a distinct fragrance, which is Jason, no doubt. I went to get aura pictures taken at a metaphysical store not long after he died. Aura is the energy field around the body. In the photo I could see someone standing next to me. I did not know the psychic who was interpreting the photo. I never told this person about Jason. Others could see a definite presence standing next to me as well. We could clearly see a person, head and shoulders, part of his torso. After the picture sat for a while, it developed more, and the figure became more of a blur. The psychic explained to me there was someone on the other side who really loved me and I loved him. I went back there several times, and every time Jason showed up in the photos.

There were times when I was feeling low—in stores or in restaurants—and the song "At Last" would come over the speakers. I knew it was him. At other times I have smelled him and knew he was nearby.

It took a while for me to move forward, and I have slowly begun dating again. About two years after his death, I had a boyfriend. It was a rather turbulent relationship, and I think Jason was around trying to get my attention away from this fellow. My garage has lots of Jason's belongings stored there. We were standing in the garage when a series of boxes started to shake. There were large boxes everywhere—a refrigerator box, and some TV boxes, all made of heavy cardboard, not something that could move with a gust of wind. Nothing else around us was shaking, so it couldn't have been an earthquake. We started thinking there was an animal in them. One by one, my boyfriend picked up the boxes and tossed them away from the pile. The garage became still, nothing happening.

A spare tire for Jason's truck sat on top of the boxes moved. While his personal belongings weren't in there, I had a load of his military gear in the garage. Looking back I think Jason was trying to warn me about the guy I was dating. He was the only guy I have really liked in the last four years, and he's the one that messed me over the worst, emotionally as well as financially.

To this day, I feel a little guilty when I date. I just hope Jason knows that I would choose him over anyone if he were here. The garage incident was crazy, to say the least. I can't believe it's been four years! He was such an amazing person; he was a great guy, and I just can't find that in boyfriends anymore.

Jason loved my kids with all his heart, even though they weren't his blood. He did not deserve to die the way he did, like a fish in a barrel, unable to even defend himself. He deserved so much better. He deserves to live on forever any way he can. He was the man who sent his sister flowers for Mother's Day.

He is not forgotten by any of his friends and families. At the funeral, the President of the United States told me that I would be taken care of. However, later the Fort Hood shooting was ruled an Act of Violence, prohibiting benefits he would have received if he had died overseas. I feel forgotten by the military. I know Jason is with me, he is my love.

"And then the spell was cast
For here we are in Heaven
At Last."

—Etta James

David and Erin

(Maj. David Yaggy, as told by his wife, Erin, and mother, Elanora)

"I'm here without you, baby,
But you're still with me in my dreams."

—Three Doors Down

Around Easter 2001, I was introduced to David by my cousin, Will Oliver, who was David's roommate. David flew the UH1-N (Huey helicopter), and became a flight instructor in the plane T-34. I was trying to reach Will, to invite him to a family Easter brunch, and David kept answering the phone. I told David to tell Will he is in trouble for not returning my calls, and David was welcome to come to the brunch too! The brunch was supposed to last only a couple of hours, but they arrived around 10 or 11 and left around 9 or 10 that evening.

We had a great time that day. A friend of my aunt who was at the brunch said, "I don't think Erin has stopped smiling. Please remember to invite me to the wedding!"

"Whatever," I told her.

I couldn't fathom that possibility. I knew he was too amazing—smart, handsome, tall, and funny. Still, I kept hoping he'd ask for my number or something. The fact that he wouldn't leave gave me plenty of encouragement, especially when my aunt said she was tired. We went down the road to a bar.

I tried to think of how I was going to see him again, but didn't want to seem forward. My friends suggested I ask my cousin (and therefore David) if they wanted to join us at a concert, so I left a message regarding our plans. I was excited to hear David's voice when he returned my call. He said he was sorry that Will was out of town and wouldn't be able to make it. I told him he was welcome to come if he didn't mind being the only guy.

David ended up meeting us, and it was so cool to have him there! We kept smiling at each other (again), but at least now he had my phone number and asked if I minded if he called me. It was history after that.

David was about to go on his first deployment, but we found time to go on many fun dates in downtown San Diego and along the coast, with lots of fun memories. We had a beautiful daughter. David went on a lot more deployments, but an accident happened in spring stateside.

My husband, Maj. David Yaggy, USMC, was a Huey helicopter pilot and T-34 flight instructor. He died on March 14, 2008, during a training mission with his student, A. J. Prezioso. They encountered bad weather and crashed into Chandler Mountain in Alabama. Our daughter, Elizabeth, was eighteen months old at the time.

That Friday afternoon, I went on a short trip to the grocery. On my return, I found two messages on the answering machine. One was from David's mother, hoping to talk to him. Another was from our realtor, she had previously admitted that she "sensed" things and said she wanted to check on "her pilots" because a plane had just crashed. This was part of what I later think of as a message of help from my husband.

I went straight to the computer and saw that a T-34 had crashed. It was not a good feeling. I called David's mom because I worried that I was missing something, and I wanted to ask her for her prayers for the family that had just lost their loved ones. I didn't think of us as part of that family.

I called the squadron but I knew they wouldn't tell me. Long story, short, I was very on edge. When I heard that knock at the door, I wasn't going to answer it. I knew that the knock was the last thing I wanted. Luckily, I saw the wheel of a stroller showing through the glass door and knew it was friends asking to go on a walk. They had not heard any news, but felt they wanted to walk with me. I asked them to help me grab the dog and baby. I grabbed the cell phone; I wanted to get out of the house and would explain in a moment. I had to get out! They told me they felt as if they needed to come and see us. I will forever be grateful that they were there. It had been a long week for them, but they felt the need to come over. I'm sure this was guided by David so that I wouldn't be alone when the news came.

I explained to my friends that a plane had crashed, and no one would tell me what was going on. I knew that it was his kind of plane, and I told them I was waiting to hear that both my husband and cousin were safe and sound on the ground.

My cousin called my phone. (I knew he was assigned to notify me.) "Where are you?" he asked.

"Why?"

"I am at your house; I need to talk to you."

I was just down the block and knew I needed to run. I started running with my daughter and the dog, but my friend realized what had happened. She was crying as she said, "No, Erin, leave her here. We have her."

I'm not sure if my feet touched the ground, but I knew they stopped working when I saw my cousin in his special uniform used for notification.

"It can't be him!"

"Yes, it is him."

"He was just hurt, okay, he was just hurt!"

"No, he was killed."

I was the one to tell David's parents. That was David's wish, that it be me and not some stranger. I now think it could have been helpful that I had called her to tell her a plane had crashed so she wasn't totally blindsided. Either way, it was the worst news to ever give someone. I won't forget the cry that came through the phone line, and I was grateful my father-in-law was there.

Here are the messages David gave to us right away. Cool, crazy things that happened afterward.

The night of the service at Pensacola, Florida, David's aunt Katherine, who was in Baltimore at the time, said she got up in the middle of the night and went into her kitchen and she saw David standing there in uniform. She was stunned, but she felt he was there because that was the last place the whole family was together for a Christmas celebration. It was a happy occasion on that Christmas.

Elanora, David's mom, shared another experience. "Growing up, David and his siblings were called the *three little turkeys*. A friend was even inspired to create a wooden cutout of a turkey to decorate their pool house. When they moved to the house David grew up in, they'd periodically see groups of wild turkeys. They hadn't seen any since the children were young." Soon after David's passing, my in-laws were driving down the long drive when three turkeys walked across the road. They haven't seen turkeys since. They felt it was David, playing a joke on them.

The Pensacola house where we lived when David died had an intricate intercom system that never worked. We finally figured out a way to make the bell work, but that was it. After David died, we heard weird noises come from it. Baby monitors in different houses made noise, even car radios. The intercom made sounds that would go on and on until someone would say, "Okay, David, that's enough." Then it would stop.

The last night we lived there before we moved away, the intercom went berserk at 2 a.m. It sounded loud and frenzied. His mother shouted from the guest room, "David, that is enough. Stop it!" It beeped twice and never made another sound.

Little things continued. David's mom, Elanora, told about yet another electronic communication. "Erin, you always said that David contacted you through the static on the radio. Periodically, the intercom system in the house in Pensacola rattled with static. In June, you all came to Baltimore for a wedding, and the radio in David's old room burst forth with static. I never heard static in that radio, so I'm sure that David was telling you how wonderful you were to come to Baltimore for the wedding!

During that period, I had a dream, a very short one. In it I heard a "bang" and saw a bright light. I am sure that David was making certain we knew how the accident happened. We were relieved, because it meant that it was very quick for him.

Sometime later, I had a dream that the altimeter in David's helicopter was not working; it was not confirmed in the investigation, as far as I know. A few months later, I woke up in tears and cried throughout the day. I was also restless, and periodically went to the computer to check the e-mail or play a game. Around midday, I opened the computer and found pictures from Christmas 2007, lots of pictures of David and me and the family, reminders of a wonderful holiday we all spent together. I had not pulled those pictures up, and no one had looked at them for quite a while. Once again, I think David was trying to find some way to say he is with us—even if we can't see or hear him.

David's mother tells of a recent happening. "We had gone to New York and you, Erin, and Corbett had a wonderful birthday party in Central Park. All of David's dad's siblings and spouses were there, too. Coming home, I was pretty weepy for some reason. I received some antidepressants from my doctor several days earlier, but I hadn't taken them. I had taken them to NYC, but never started them. On the way home I vowed to start the pills that night. We arrived home, unpacked, and had dinner. I went up to get ready for bed and I got the pills out, but I noticed there were four pills laid out in a straight line, with military precision. The instructions were to take a half pill for the first eight days, which I hadn't done; I would never have put them in a straight line. I think it was David's way of telling me, 'Get a grip, Mom!'"

Things didn't happen for about a year and a half, and one day I was fussing with David about not being around. I went to the grocery store one afternoon, and when I came out, there sitting on the console of the gearshift was a small seashell. We had all gone to the beach that first summer after he died, and when we went to Arlington on our return, we place many seashells and sharks' teeth on his grave. Again, it was a gentle reminder that he is here with us.

The Christmas of 2011 for some reason was a hard one for me and for David's dad. The day we were leaving for New York, I was cleaning the kitchen counter and found a seashell on it. I can't guarantee that it wasn't there before, but I don't think so. I felt like our David was with us that Christmas, and I carried the shell with me everywhere.

We all seem to find head's-up pennies when we are having a rough day. A. J., David's student who also died, wore the number four as his sports team number (the school officials retired his jersey at his high school). When I told Elanora, David's mother, that we had heard weird intercom noises, she confided she saw A. J., not David, in his dress uniform standing in her kitchen the night she found out that they had died. His mom finds (no kidding) four pennies when she is out and about. If I hadn't been with her when my daughter found a head's-up penny, followed by three more in the same area, I might not have believed it. I get that pennies have a 50/50 chance of being head's up, but I wasn't sure about people always dropping four pennies.

My daughter, a first grader, was selected to introduce General Dempsey at a TAPS Gala in DC, in the spring of 2014. We arrived from Baltimore and went right to a rehearsal for the event at 4:30 p.m. I called to make sure we didn't need to be dressed, and the representative for the event said, "It will be fine, just show up at 4:30."

We went to the rehearsal and the organizers asked us why we were not dressed. We had eight minutes to get back to the hotel and get dressed. I was totally panicked until we got in the car and my daughter said, "Look, Mom! Daddy! There's a penny on the floor of the elevator; it's from Dad." At that moment I just took a deep breath and knew it was David, saying, "Be calm."

I have had further experiences, some with rainbows. Sometimes I wonder about something and find someone who knows the answer to the wondering. There are so many times this has happened—some people call them *Godwinks*—I think of them as David helping me out.

I have seen rainbows on days that have been very hard. One of our close friends, Sam, died a year and a half after my husband, in a plane/ helicopter crash. I was at Home Depot (my husband's second *home*), and realized the store had lowered their flag to half-mast for our friend Sam. It meant so much that they had given him that honor; as I looked up, the cloud moved and there was a very distinct rainbow. It would be very much like these two guys to do something like that as a joke too. They were sending me a smile, and their favorite Home Depot was at the end of the rainbow.

Invitations have come to me at unexpected times, when my heart was really sinking, amazing invitations to go to White House functions or to join veterans who sing before Ravens home games in Baltimore. I feel David is guiding these moments for me.

David and Erin

How Often Your Heart Drops Pennies from Heaven

Each day found, in the car, on the counter,

In the elevator, on your grave,

I see lovers walking silently on sidewalks,

Pennies shine on dark and sunny days,

I know it is you, smiling, hugging,

Kissing me from heaven.

—Maureen McGill

Heroes are with us ... Always

Support Links

http://patrickmccaffreyfoundation.org/Patricks_House.html

http://www.farmvetco.org/

http://iands.org/home.html

http://www.VeteranVillages.org

http://www.washingtonwarriorwidows.org/

http://www.vietnamexp.com/McDonald/abouttheauthor.htm

http://www.taps.org/

http://www.woundedwarriorproject.org/

http://www.mwsadispatches.com

Acknowledgments

Thank you to all who contributed to the memory of these heroes. Deepest gratitude to the widows, parents, children, and friends who share loving messages that continue to reach us every day.

Thank you to those who supported and contributed to this collection of stories: Val Dumond, Nadia McCaffrey, Theresa Morehead, the Reverend Bill McDonald, International Association of Near Death Studies, Kimberly Clark Sharp, Seattle IANDS, Debbie Upton, Andrew Dee, Jeffrey Pittle, and Ava Seal.

For more information about any of the titles published by Ozark Mountain Publishing, LLC, soon to be released titles, or other items in our catalog, write, phone or visit our website:

Ozark Mountain Publishing, LLC

PO Box 754

Huntsville, AR 72740

479-738-2348/800-935-0045

www.ozarkmt.com

About the Author

Maureen McGill, MA, BFA, has been an associate professor of theatre and dance at Pacific Lutheran University in Tacoma, Washington, for thirty-eight years. She directed the University Dance Ensemble and taught courses in dance, movement, choreography, and healing arts.

Maureen's keen interest in the intuitive arts has expanded her curiosity to the spiritual side of life. She is a featured reader of tarot in the Northwest and appears at Intuitive Arts Fairs in the Seattle region. As a frequent guest on local and international radio networks, her work has opened doors to the use of symbols and metaphors to help those in the midst of loss and grief to find light. "It is a positive experience to share in the healing messages of the tarot," she says.

Maureen and coauthor Nola Davis wrote *Live from the Other Side* (Ozark Mountain Publishing, 2010), a collection of real-life stories of communication from the other side.

Maureen is an active member of the International Association of Near Death Studies and presented at the 2014 IANDS conference in Newport Beach, California. She is a member of the Military Writers Society of America.

Inspired by the theme of military loss, Maureen compiled *Baby, It's You*, a collection of real experiences from military widows, mothers, family members, friends, and surviving heroes. In these stories, the other side brings messages of hope and inspiration, demystifying death and after-life experiences. A beautiful video inspired by this book was produced in collaboration with Jeffrey Pittle, creative director, which she shares at book presentations.

Maureen enjoys the beauty of the Pacific Northwest where she lives.

For more information go to:

https://www.facebook.com/pages/Baby-Its-You-Messages-From-Deceased-Heroes/594079927390390?ref=aymt_homepage_panel.

E-mail: messagesfromheroes@gmail.com.